HISTORY

OF THE

MORAVIAN CHURCH

IN

PHILADELPHIA.

(Fac Simile)

HISTORY

OF THE

MORAVIAN CHURCH

IN

PHILADELPHIA,

FROM

ITS FOUNDATION IN 1742 TO THE PRESENT TIME.

COMPRISING NOTICES, DEFENSIVE OF ITS
FOUNDER AND PATRON,

COUNT NICHOLAS LUDWIG VON ZINZENDORFF.

TOGETHER WITH AN APPENDIX.

BY

ABRAHAM RITTER.

PHILADELPHIA:
PUBLISHED BY HAYES & ZELL.
1857.

C. SHERMAN & SON, PRINTERS,

19 St. James Street.

TESTIMONIALS.

Brother Abraham Ritter submits to me three drawings, which he intends to have engraved and published, as illustrative of a history, which he is writing, of the Brethren's Church in Philadelphia. I have carefully examined those drawings, and have no hesitancy in giving this assurance,—that each and every one of them is an accurate and faithful representation of the several parts of the several buildings erected by the United Brethren in Philadelphia, as places of worship, for the residence of the congregational minister, and for the accommodation of such of the brethren and sisters as business might call to Philadelphia, for a short time. Those buildings were on the southeast corner of Race Street and Moravian Alley—now called Bread Street. I have always understood that these buildings were all erected about the year 1742; and I know they were taken down in 1819.

No. 1, The Exterior of the Church, and the Parsonage attached, in which the elders of the Church met on business, and in which there was public worship and congregational meetings.

No. 2, represents the Lower, or Audience-Room, for public worship, in the same Church; and

No. 3, is a view of the Upper Room or Hall of the old Moravian Church.

JOHN BINNS.

PHILADELPHIA, July 9th, 1856.

I HAVE examined the drawings of the Interior and Exterior of the original Moravian Church in Philadelphia; all of which—having been an early member, and regular worshipper in the said building—I am happy to confirm as truthful and characteristic recollections of that edifice.

GEORGE ESLER.

PHILADELPHIA, Aug. 28th, 1856.

PREFACE.

WERE it for the mere pleasure of writing a book, or the evaporative fame of authorship, the contents of this volume would have slept in the unexplored bosom of its fathers; yet there is a motive, a design, and a pleasure in the research, inasmuch as the lights and shades of antiquity may be elicited to refresh the memory of the centenarian, or enlighten the wonderings of the satchelled youth, or the full-fledged collegian.

There, is, however, in this, as there is doubtless in all communities, a portion of our race for whom oblivion would seem to have been permitted, who pass every yesterday of their existence, and that of their ancestors, as though Time had but just marked their being, and the "everlasting *now*" was the necessary absorbent of all that life holds dear.

'Tis well, however, for our day and its succession, that the germs of antiquity *will* sprout, from time to time, and bud, blossom, and bloom, under the fructifying influences of its bedewing patronage; and well, too, for history and its cravings, that there are lovers of dusty records, prone to sweep their pages, and present and compare the past with the present, by the autographic details of "the things that were."

My motive, therefore, is to gather, from the dust of oblivion, the atoms of a venerable centre, remould the dignity of an ancient pile, and present it, its constituents, and its successors, to the heirs and representatives of their early fathers, as well as to the antiquarian spirit of the present, or the future age.

My design is to call up the spirit of our fathers, to chasten our own waywardness, to simplify our manners, to imbue us with their faith and faithfulness, to qualify our practices—else endangered by modernized Christianity—to elasticize a more apostolic atmosphere, and to offer St. Paul's call upon the Philippians, 3 : 17, "Brethren, be ye followers together of me, and mark them which walk so, as ye have us for an ensample."

Although considerably beyond the meridian of life, I have abundant cause for gratitude to my merciful Providence, for the freshness of all my faculties; my "eye is not satisfied with seeing, nor my ear with hearing;" hence, a retrospect of my own times, and a social fondling with the times of our predecessors, is a pleasure remunerative in its issues, and sufficiently so to protect me from the charge of vanity, too often appurtenant to authorship.

In thus offering my gatherings to the public, I am

happy to say that they are neither indebted to fancy for lights, nor to imagination for shades; the plain matter-of-fact accompanies the representation of the origin of the reminiscence, and the attest being by two competent contemporaneous eye-witnesses, ought, at least, to be guarantees for credulity.

Under the artistic and skilful hand of our townsman, Mr. Edward F. Durang—whose ready mind and quick conception caught up my dots and lines—memory is embodied, and speech to the eye enforced, from the *fac simile* of a speck of a hundred and more years ago.

His delineations of both the exterior and the interior of the "old Moravian Church," are truthful to a line; which, though drawn from early impressions, deepened by continuous associations, ripened by time, and warmed into resuscitation in the bosom of an antiquarian spirit, are still the accurate architectural *remodelling of his hands*, graphic beyond cavil, and fresh as to an eye-witness; to this let the testimonials speak.

The portraits of the bishops, &c., are equally reliable, being from the original canvas in the conservatory in Herrnhuth.

In reference to my review of the letters of James Logan, the opinion of Kalm, the Swedish traveller, and their indorsement nearly one hundred years after their date, by their furtherance to posterity in the "Annals of Philadelphia," by John F. Watson, I have but to remark, that the indignity inflicted upon the memory of Count Zinzendorff, his highly respectable descendants, and the spiritual fruit of his labors, ripe and ripening to Christian perfection, has voluntarily and unprovokedly thrown off the mantle of qualification, bared its offensive front to the *ad libitum* repulse of a respectable Christian community, and cannot complain if severity tips the thong that reaches the source of the evil.

Yet I set nothing down in malice; but honest Christian zeal, grown to an extensive evidence of good sound sense—else impugned—is justly entitled to a champion.

For the rest, I offer the volume as a link of time to time, and perpetuity to the manes of departed worth.

THE AUTHOR.

CONTENTS.

CHAPTER XV.

CHAPTER XVI.

CHAPTER XVII.

CHAPTER XVIII.

CHAPTER XIX.

CHAPTER XX.

CHAPTER XXI.

CHAPTER XXII.

CHAPTER XXIII.

CHAPTER XXIV.

CHAPTER XXV.

APPENDIX.

CHAPTER I.

CHAPTER II.

CHAPTER III.

CHAPTER IV.

CONCLUSION.

ILLUSTRATIONS.

INTRODUCTION.

If Time disaggregates material, it does not deny a compensatory medium to the association of the past with the future; nor can it, for if even records fail, Memory, invigorated by age, and strengthened by exercise, comes to the rescue, lights up the past, and rejuvenates amongst the ruins, or their shades, of the wisdom of our early fathers!

History is the handmaid of Time. But for it, the things that were, would be smothered in the dust of oblivion, or their manes scattered, to be gathered only by the already impervious cloud that hangs tauntingly over the past; hence, to link time to time, and gather up the crumbs of its early forbearance, I venture upon the ocean of recollection, and offer from its bosom the floating components of a part, at least, of the dignity of its day!

My object is not merely to amuse with flights of fancy, or tints of fitful imagination, but in very truth and soberness, to tax the throne of observation, call up the energies of reflection, and present the fruits from memory's grafts as nursed and nurtured by the irrigation of tradition, as well as from the garner of winnowed gatherings. But Data, too, are before me, and Records are imperious; but Memory—jealous of its prerogative—may not be impugned, seeing that contemporaneous attest confirms its portrait.

The First Moravian Church in Philadelphia, even then a colony of Great Britain, is certainly not the least of her sisters in our great city's ancient landmarks; but, on the contrary, has indubitable claims to a respectful reference, as well for her unpretending structure, as such, as for the labors of her love as a pioneer in the vineyard of Him, who commanded his disciples to go and work in it.

HISTORY

OF

THE MORAVIAN CHURCH

IN PHILADELPHIA.

CHAPTER I.

The Right Rev. Nicholas Lewis von Zinzendorff—Some account of the object of his visit to America.

AMONGST the annals of 1742, the debut of Count Zinzendorff to this, from foreign climes, may not be considered the least of the events of that day.

He came, not as a mere adventurer, not as a time-killing wanderer, nor as a visionary fanatic, to gratify a morbid appetite for fame, but to give vent to the abundance of his heart in another sphere, and under the impulse of the Spirit of God, as far as in him lay, further the Gospel of Jesus Christ, plant his faith as a grain of mustard-seed, and water it with the dews of prayer and supplication.

This gentleman was the son of George Lewis, Count Zinzendorff, and born in Dresden, on the 26th of May, A.D. 1700.

His father was a premier of the court of Saxony, but withal a pious and devoted servant of God, a member of the Lutheran Church; and his son was baptized in that faith; but subsequently, about A.D. 1723, became one of four United Brethren, at Berthelsdorf; and on May 12th, 1724, was present at, and took part in laying the corner-stone of the church at Herrnhuth.

Although much engaged in temporal affairs, he devoted all his leisure to the cause of his Divine Master; serving in and out of the Church, wherever and in whatever precept, example, counsel, or exhortation, could be beneficially applied. But, in order to further his usefulness—being fully prepared—he applied for ordination, and A.D. 1734, was ordained, and entered as one of the ministry of the Moravian Church.

In 1737, he was consecrated Bishop of the Church, by the Bishops Daniel Ernst Jablousky, and David Nitchman, and by consent and proxy of Bishop Sitkovius, of Lissa, in Poland, who writes, that "He would not only gladly and willingly contribute his vote in writing to the proposed ordination of the Count, but though absent, yet present in spirit, instead of the imposition of his hands, would confirm it with his own handwriting and signature," &c. &c.—Spangenberg's Life of Zinzendorff, p. 233.

"His ecclesiastical functions were Bishop, Advocate, Ordinary, and Representative, with full powers, of the Church of the Bohemian and Moravian Brethren, adhering to the Augsburg Confession."—Latrobe's Preface to Spangenberg's Life of Zinzendorff, p. vi.

Notwithstanding the advantages of his birth, education, associations, and wealth, his single eye to the glory of God, forgetting those things that were behind, he reached forth unto those things that were before, and like the great Apostle, pressed toward the mark of his calling of God in Christ Jesus; and to this end, laying off his episcopal honors for a season, he came forth from home, as an Ordinarius, with a few followers of a like-minded missionary spirit, to reach and teach, to gather and instruct his scattered German brethren, as also the Indians in North America, becoming "all things to all men, that he might, by all means, save some."

He arrived in New York, in the month of November, 1741; whence, after visiting some friends in Long Island, whose acquaintance he had made in St. Thomas, he came to Philadelphia, where, after being the guest of the late venerable John Stephen Benezet (of whose pedigree more in the Appendix), he hired a house, in which he held regular religious services for his immediate adherents, and any others who might feel inclined to avail themselves of these means of grace.

In advance of this, however, he wrote to Gov. Thomas, of the Province, requesting him to send some one who was acquainted with both English and German, to be present at his meetings, in order to test his orthodoxy and avert suspicion of his purpose; thus, showing himself freely subject to the powers that be.

Having preached in various places, but for a season located in Germantown, in and about Philadelphia,* he settled down for the Lutherans, whose pastor he continued to be for about nine months; but differences of opinion arising between him and them, or some of them, he withdrew from their service, and with thirty-four of his adherents formed the Moravian Society, according to

* See Life of Zinzendorff by the Rev. August Gottlieb Spangenberg, published in London, 1838.

their original tenets; which gave rise to the edifice, long since scattered in atoms, but now to be represented in its original, simple, and unpretending form, feature, and expression.

It is not, however, my purpose to write the Life and Character of Zinzendorff: that is already before the world, from abler hands, and which has furnished me with the foregoing portrait, besides abundant rebutting evidences against the aspersions, misconceptions, and misconstruction of his religious zeal; nor can I conceal my pleasure, in the opportunity thus offered, to meet the objections of James Logan, Kalm, and others, as set forth in Watson's Annals; as well as my grateful emotions in being one of the many, permitted to lodge in the branches of the tree of his planting, and to enjoy the fragrance of its fruitful bearing; not, however as a bigot to sectarianism, nor an exclusive to any other Christian denomination; for God hath said from the beginning: "In all places where I record my name, I will come unto thee, and I will bless thee" (Exod. 20, 24); and that he has recorded that Holy Name "from the rising of the sun, even unto the going down of the same," where "incense is offered as a pure offering," is even now a glorious testimony to the infallibility of his word, Christianity itself being the pure offering, differing in form, but not in fact; not in the incense, but in the censer only, that wafts it to the throne of his acceptance; "for with the heart man believeth unto righteousness, and with the mouth confession is made unto salvation." (Romans 10: 10.)

In advance, however, of my history, it will be but common justice to its origin, to brush from the skirts of Zinzendorff the spots and the wrinkles blemishing his fair fame,—there placed by those who could not, or would not, understand him ; and whilst I

> "Their unlucky deeds relate,
> Shall nothing extenuate,
> Nor set down aught in malice,"

but with honest, yet earnest candor, offer a palliative to the opprobrium, and a shield to the thrusts, so unjustly, if not wantonly, aimed at his character for purity and good behavior.

CHAPTER II.

Watson's Annals versus Count Zinzendorff, and defence against unjust accusations.

As History is the handmaid of Time, Time ought to be a veracious chronicler, not only of matters and things, but of men and manners; and when this handmaid offers her gatherings, it is but meet that she should do so well savored with civility in the preparation for the great public ordinary.

Men and manners are important items in history, tenacious of their due, and jealous of an unbiassed furtherance to future generations; because far and wide goes their fame, and whether for good or evil, an indelible impression either wrinkles or tints the memory of the subject portrayed.

Watson's Annals is a very laudable enterprise, and of deservedly popular issue. It has also taken its place in the *bibliothèque* of the literati, and holds the praise or the censure of many of "such as were;" amongst whom the founder and patron of the original Church of the Moravian Brethren in Philadelphia, seems not to have been sufficiently popular for the author's reasonably liberal or even qualified estimate. And I must declare in the outset, that had Mr. Watson taken half the pains to cater for Zinzendorff, that he did for James Logan and others, the contrast would have been less offensive to his followers, and more creditable to the author.

On page 541, vol. i, after announcing the arrival of the Count, and dipping him at once into a "pool" of doubtful reputation for sanity, and reviewing him at least as an oddity, Mr. Watson offers, in confirmation, a letter from him, of 1741–2, to the parents of some young females of his congregation, who were evidently opposed to his ministration, as well as to the adhesion of their daughters to his spiritual guidance.

"To THE COOPER, F. VENDE, GERMANTOWN.

"I take you, both man and wife, to be notoriously children of the devil, and you, the woman, to be a twofold child of hell; yet I would have your damnation as tolerable as possible. The laws provide against such unreasonable parents, and will not suffer you to keep your daughter against her consent. You may vex her soul, if that sevenfold devil which possesseth you will permit. Then consider, and leave your daughter to the congregation."

Again, to NEUMAN, he writes:

"In case you die without forcing your daughter away, your former sin shall be forgiven you; but if you resume your murdering spirit against her soul, by her consent or not, I recall my peace, and you I leave to the devil; and the curse of your child—thereby lost—shall rest on you till she is redeemed. Amen."

Watson adds: "This is really very curious supremacy, as well as theology. Miss L. and Miss V., much against the will of their families, went off to Germany."

Differing with Mr. Watson in his conclusions, it is but common justice to the author of this "curiosity," to consider his position as the father of a Christian gathering, his jealous care of his converts, "his enthusiasm in the cause of his Master, common to almost every soul at its relief from the burden of sin," the spirited zeal of the man, and the forceful idiom of his native tongue. The "supremacy," I presume, consists in the strength of his language.

The German language is as forceful as it is comprehensive. Its imprecations can be concentrated, and spent in powerful issues, and the severity of its denunciatory powers reach the lethargy of its subjects. But deep as may be the infliction upon his sensibilities, his accustomed ear would not writhe at the application; whereas literally given in English, trained to the sound and sense of its own vocabulary, the hearer or reader, ignorant of the German idiom, might think it harsh, and perhaps irreconcilable to his own mode of expression; and this I suppose to be the cause of Mr. Watson's view of the Count's supremacy.

The pastor spoke from the fulness of his heart, impelled by the jealousy of his zeal, and strove against the temporal power, that he thought was infringing or annulling his spiritual gains. He spoke in the tongue best intelligible to his opponents; their own native, comprehensive, and comprehensible idiom, which to them doubtless was less curious than impressive.

His theology, however, is even less vulnerable, for although its curiousness appears to be derived from the application of terms, yet its defence, or, at least, its parallel, offers itself in Holy Writ:

"Woe unto you, Scribes, Pharisees, hypocrites! for ye compass sea and land to make one proselyte, and when he is made, ye make him twofold more the child of hell than yourselves." So said our Saviour (Matthew 23 : 15) to the opponents of his work.

And of St. Paul (Acts 13 : 8, 9, 10) having an untoward subject before him, we read thus:

"But Elymas, the sorcerer, withstood them, seeking to turn away the deputy from the faith."

"Then Paul, filled with the Holy Ghost, set his eyes on him, and said, O full of all subtlety and mischief, thou child of the devil! thou enemy of all righteousness! wilt thou not cease to pervert the right ways of the Lord? And now, behold, the hand of the Lord is upon thee, and thou shalt be blind, not seeing the sun for a season."

Without making a St. Paul of our Zinzendorff, though he may have been as good a man, it certainly will not be any strain of the point, to place them upon the same footing in their mission, and accord to them equal indulgence in their mode or language of rebuke to untoward subjects. Argument will scarcely be necessary to obtain this concession. We may, therefore, ask, wherein consists "the curious supremacy and theology" of Zinzendorff's German, more than in St. Paul's Greek?

But if language equally severe has sped from the pulpit of our day, why marvel at the issues of a century ago!

A very venerable and pious herald of the Cross, within this century, rang the welkin of old "St. George's," in North Fourth Street of our city, with the most powerful invectives against sin and sinners, and once said that "Some of them would not believe, unless they were shaken over the pit of hell."

Now, although these exemplars may be deemed wanting in refinement, yet we should remember that the obduracy of the natural man cannot always be impressed by the etiquette of parlor *politesse;* and whilst some may be successfully chastised with whips, others require scorpions!

We next come to Kalm, the Swedish traveller, whose *ipse dixit* Mr. W., p. 542, same volume, thus offers:

"Kalm, the Swedish traveller, here in 1748, says, 'His uncommon behavior here, persuaded many Englishmen of rank, that he was diseased in his head.'"

The total absence of the consideration for this allusion, renders the whole paragraph nugatory, and not available to any adverse conception; but as we have positive testimony to the contrary, it will be but due to his character to give it.

Nor is it a little remarkable that the venerable Spangenberg, his contemporary and biographer, had unwittingly anticipated a direct provision for such an assumption in his intercourse with Zinzendorff and his friends, twelve years before "Kalm's Report," to wit, in 1736.

On page 217 of "Spangenberg's Life of Zinzendorff," speaking of his sojourn in Revel, in Russia, he writes: "Many persons of rank were uncommonly attached to him, and reflected whether there were no means of retaining him in the country. He was also urgently requested to preach in the Cathedral Church, which he did, on the following Wednesday."

The Cathedral was uncommonly full of persons of all classes, and the people said, "If all sermons were like this, all men would be converted."

There does not appear to have been any "disease in his head" at this time, and we have never read or heard of any since. On the contrary, in 1748, when Kalm wrote, much of his natural eccentricity had merged in his own review, and passed into a more modified course. Still, in justice to Kalm, or perhaps more particularly his "Englishmen of rank," it may be but proper to suggest a contrast between the general character of the Germans and the English, especially as exhibiting its full force in a temperament like that of Zinzendorff's, of active energy, rapidity of thought and utterance, and indomitable zeal, clad in national peculiarities, the lack of qualification in the critic, unwilling or unwitting, might cause an oblique view of national prejudice.

That Zinzendorff was eccentric, his best friends do not deny; but it was natural and not assumed, and in him, the fault of genius. Now, although eccentricity may be, and often is, put on for the occasion, to pass for wit, or to furbish some rusty coin of literary lore, or is too often assumed as a current to popularity, nay even worse, to pass idiocy for common sense, and downright derangement for wisdom, yet the general issues of Zinzendorff, whether moral or religious, his life, his labors, and the thousand and one evidences of mind, memory, and understanding, in their fruits, ought ever to be a panoply of justice to his memory, and a shield against the thrusts of error and misunderstanding.

But to proceed.

Our historian, same vol. p. 542, rather deepens the shades into which the preceding *exposé* thrusts the subject of their animadversion, and clothes him in the rags and tatters of mental mendicity, or decorates him with the fancied implements of Quixotic chivalry; to which end the letter of James Logan reads as follows, which I give *verbatim et literatim*, because it is but too vulnerable in all its parts, "and I intend to meet it according to its deserts."

"A MS. letter of James Logan, of the year 1743, written in confidential frankness to a friend, speaks of the Count as follows:

"I have had frequent intercourse with him, and heartily wish I could say anything concerning him to satisfaction; but his conduct lost him all credit here, being now only regarded by his own few Moravians.

"He sent to the Friend's Meeting a letter signed Anne, the Elder, written in an odd French style, which it was difficult to put into any consistent meaning or sense. About the same time he framed an instrument of resignation of all his honors and dignities to some relative. This was done in Latin, but still more odd than his French; in some parts carrying a show of elegance, but in other parts mere nonsense; in other places plain enough, and in others perfectly unintelligible. This he desired me to put in English. As it could not, he had it printed as it was in Latin, and invited the Governor and all who understood Latin to meet him. Several met, when he read off his instrument, giving each of them a printed copy; but after all this parade, he withdrew his papers and himself too, saying, 'On reflection, he must first advise with some of his friends in Germany.' This conduct astonished the company, who generally concluded him insane. He had lately been visiting the Iroquois. In short, he appears a mere knight-errant in religion, scarce less than Don Quixote was in chivalry. Other facts of his singular behavior are mentioned by Logan. I have preserved some other facts, respecting his strange conduct in Germantown. Very wild notions are imputed to him, and told, in detail, by Rimius, of Prussia, who printed a book of it in London, in 1753. The decree of George III, as Elector of Hanover, against them, and which induced them to come to Pennsylvania, see in the Pennsylvania Journal, of the 20th of December, 1750."

Here we have an uncompromising and unqualified tirade against the education, the sanity, and the common sense of the Count!

It is fortunate for Zinzendorff's few Moravians that Logan's dictum is not gospel; and vastly marvellous that, after his labors of a whole year in and about Philadelphia, with a growing popularity, deducible even from the letter "to the Cooper," and "Logan's frequent intercourse" with him, that he could not "find anything concerning him satisfactory."

"Being only regarded by his few Moravians," Mr. Logan might have allowed him to be beloved, and given him his increase, since, in 1743, he had grown in the affections of his immediate followers, and joined by others, and was evidently more than regarded, seeing that an ordinary regard, a cool, calculating estimate of his worth, could never have kept these pioneers at work, under the impetus of his suggestions.

To this point, his venerable biographer writes: "He then proceeded to Philadelphia, devoted himself as much as the time permitted to his beloved Lutherans, who were also much attached to him, and established a church, consisting of those Englishmen who had recently been brought by the ministry of the Brethren to a knowledge of the Gospel."

And again: "Finally, he preached in the evening of the 31st of December, O. S., on the eve of his departure, in the newly erected Moravian Church, in Philadelphia. During the sermon, his numerous audience were much affected. He left the church before the conclusion of the service, to avoid the pain of taking leave of so many persons."

Such was the regard of his few Moravians at the very time (1743) when James Logan wrote.

Under such testimony, can it be a matter of wonder if we ask, where could James Logan have been at this time? Can it be possible, that in this mere village he could have been ignorant of a light shining in so small a space, whose rays might have scorched his borders! Alas, for an unwilling witness!

But, the Count wrote two documents, one in French, and one in Latin, both incomprehensible to him!

An unwilling witness and a biassed judge, are two very great obstacles to a fair decision. And it is not a little strange, that Logan, who claimed to rank with the literati, should have been ignorant of or blind to the educational advantages of Zinzendorff.

He was born, educated, and travelled, where French and Latin were the common currency of thought; his practice, therefore, if even his scholastic attainments had failed him, would have been a credible pass to his scholarship; besides, as a German, his national inheritance rendered the adoption of almost any foreign tongue more of a luxury than a task to his natural facilities.

The Germans in general are *recherché*. They are excellent linguists, especially in Latin and French. The better class speak these languages fluently. The German scholar thinks in them, and when he writes he embodies his thoughts in them, and presents them as the currency of his mind.

Zinzendorff was a man of many languages; supplying thought with terms as it sped from his very rapid conceptions, and traced them to the eye, from his varied powers of speech. Latin, German, or French, were alike to him, and therefore, if these documents were unintelligible to his accuser, they must have been so from the rapidity of his thoughts, supplied in terms, or couched in the tongue of their conception; perhaps, beyond the limits of Logan or obnoxious to his kindly considerations of patience and forbearance; and in this view of that matter, I am happy to find I am ably supported by Bishop Spangenberg, whom I have consulted, on page 27–8 of his Preface to his Life of Zinzendorff, where he testifies as follows:

"His style and diction were peculiarly his own. His ordinary German was anything but pure, being intermixed with a host of words and phrases derived from the French, English, Latin, and other tongues."

"Yet, notwithstanding this extraordinary feature, I must confess," observes Müller, "that his language on the whole pleases me exceedingly. It is colloquial in a high degree, but corresponds as closely to his thoughts as a moistened cloth does to the form of the human body; so that it is difficult to say how the same ideas could be differently expressed,—the chief characteristic, in my opinion, of a good style. The more original the conceptions, the more unusual will be the phraseology. And there is not one of his literary productions which does not exhibit traces more or less obvious of genius and originality.

"Whenever he professes to write pure German, he writes admirably, according to the judgment of modern critics."—Müller's Bekentnisse, pp. 3, 4.

This part of Logan's famous letter, therefore, must shrink into the deep shades of suspicion, and plead prejudice for its conception, under such rebutting testimony. The wonder is, how it could have escaped the eye of Watson, when he gave the Logan Letter to his "Annals," without a single ray from the light of other minds; but of this, hereafter.

The finale of the letter sharpens in severity, and the Count is proclaimed, in effect, a *dérangé*.

"In short," says he, "he appears a mere knight-errant in religion, scarce less than Don Quixote was in chivalry;" a most wonderful terminus of the mental labors of Logan *versus* Zinzendorff; a sad inheritance to his offspring, and a lamentable legacy to the American Moravian Church. But, thank God, our madhouses are not yet, nor are our asylums, to calm the flights of Quixotic imagination, even in embryo! And here, I might rest, and muse over Logan's toil to concentrate the bitterness of his asperity (as unworthy of comment), pierced into shades of shame and confusion, by the reflected rays from the helmet of his Don Quixote; but the perpetuity of the reflection has gone forth as a text of history, and although futile in fact, is mischievous in effect.

But controversy is unnecessary. If we refer to the counsel of Zinzendorff, it stands, because "it is of God." If to the fruits of his doings, our atmosphere is redolent of its sweet-smelling savor; for, "by their fruits, shall ye know them."

"Paul, thou art beside thyself," said Festus. "Zinzendorff, thou art a very Don Quixote," says Logan. Of this, let the reader judge.

That Logan and Zinzendorff were men of very different temperament is obvious,—the one, calm, calculating, and measured in thought and action; the other, restive, pressing to his mark, energetic in speech and decision. They were evidently as opposite in their pursuits in life. Zinzendorff sacrificed dollars and cents at the shrine of his altar, and certainly obtained thereby "a good report;" whilst Logan seems to have had another shrine; and Watson quotes thus of Logan, vol. ii, p. 524–5: "When he was a young man, and secretary to Penn, he felt an indifference to money, and deemed this a happy retirement for the cultivating of the Christian graces; but after he had some experience in life, finding how little respect and influence could be usefully exerted without such competency as to give a man ready access to good society, he thenceforth set himself seriously to endeavor, by engagements in commerce, to attain that consequence and weight which property so readily confers," as the sacrifice to his.

Leaving each to his choice, the comparison and deduction gives Zinzendorff position, without money; whilst Logan appears to have compromised his "Christian graces" for the glitter of wealth, to illumine his way to the "respect and influence" of good society.

Having thus necessarily noticed the letter, and its tendency, of James Logan, as well a prerogative as a duty to the character of the sequel of this book (but in so doing, drawn to the conclusion by its tone and tenor of a prejudiced writer), I find my opinion fully confirmed by a German author, Löhr, in his "*Geschichte u Zustände die Deutchen in Amerika*," pp. 75, 77, 86, 87, where he writes as follows, quoting Logan:

"In 1717, a great number of people from the Palatinate have, of late, immigrated to this country; they have come without recommendation, a source of great anxiety. These strangers do not suit amongst us, as the English."

In 1729, in a letter to Penn, he thus denounces them:

"The Germans," says he, "are impudent and poor strangers, of whom many have served as soldiers. They generally sought out the best tracts, and took possession of them as public property.

"When examined as to their right and title, they replied, that in Europe the general report was, that emigrants were wanted, and that there was land in abundance for them." And in 1724, he expressed great uneasiness lest "the great number should, *vi et armis*, possess the land;" but, in 1726, his fears increase, and he says, "They are a people with whom it is difficult to have intercourse; the men are well armed, and always ready for battle."

Again. "Six hundred men are expected, and if Parliament does not forbid their immigration, the colonies will be lost to the English Crown!"

Now, here is abundant evidence of the feverish pulse of Logan floating ignes fatui from his imagination, and wresting from its throne the balancing power of a sound judgment. Fancy fights must have been before him, and the fear of invasion and foreign power behind him.

Temporal usurpation seems to have worn upon him first, and the spiritual incursion of Zinzendorff capped the climax of his fears; and the whole was seethed, by the heat of his opposition, into the very dregs of prejudice. Even so, for the tirade against the Germans is as untrue as it is unjust; seeing that a more industrious, indefatigable, and economical people exists nowhere on the globe. A people, whose characteristic is economy; whose motto is economy; and who, connecting it with labor, have ever proved it to be wealth.

Their genius, mechanical and agricultural, is proverbial, and being national, must have been known in Logan's time, in proportion to what they are now; and they were so, as testified by Jonathan Dickinson, who, in 1719, writes as follows:

"We are expecting daily vessels from London with six or seven thousand Germans (Pfälzer), of whom we have had a great number about five years ago, who bought land, and settled some sixty miles west of Philadelphia, and have peaceably and industriously cultivated and improved their lands;" page 73, Löhr.

These chroniclers of their time, were both highly respectable gentlemen, and yet, this difference of report on the same subject, bears hard upon Logan's denunciation of Zinzendorff, and voluntarily confirms the charge of a mind prejudiced against the Germans and their character.

Having thus reviewed Mr. Logan's antisympathetic opinions of Zinzendorff and his countrymen, it is but natural to turn to the perpetuating medium, or its author, of the opinions, in wonder at the apathy that induced their unqualified indorsement.

Had the Moravian Church been extinguished with the mortal existence of its patron, or were it now wallowing in a slough of doubtful disputations on the soundness of his mind—had the one hundred years preceding the issue, offered nothing but oblivion to the search or common inquiry of Mr. Watson, or the memory of Zinzendorff been shattered to atoms by the maddened bruit of a lunatic asylum—had he never read, heard, or thought of the existence of a Moravian Church in Philadelphia, or been ignorant of its members, their doings, their respectability, and their continued furtherance of Zinzendorff's early, laudable, and, under God, successful labors—then might he have safely handed to posterity the unmitigated censure and opprobrium of Zinzendorff as a Quixotic pretender to Christian valor, as well as a pedantic hero of scholastic folly.

But it would be injustice to Mr. Watson to assume all this.

One hundred years had elapsed. The green bay tree of his planting had matured to a dignified diameter; its branches were widely extended; its foliage perennial, and ever fresh; its buds, blossoms, and flowers, redolent of a sweet-smelling savor, and its fame world-wide.

The Moravian Church and its missions have never been hid "under a bushel;" and yet Mr. Watson, who compassed sea and land to gather the pedigree of Logan, and ploughed the fallow ground of England, Sweden, and Prussia, to embellish his opinions of, but derogatory to Zinzendorf, withal seems not to have found anything satisfactory concerning him,—a most wonderful apathy; for, admitting for the moment the plea of misconception of Logan as a contemporary, Moravians, Moravianism, and its root in America, were certainly no enigmas when Watson indorsed Logan.

Let the historian's motto be, "Fiat justitia, ruat cœlum."

In concluding this part of my introduction, it may not

be out of place to remark, that derangement, in whatever form it may have seated itself, whether in the vivacious fancy of a Don Quixote, or the mothy sluggishness of melancholy, very seldom yields to remote generations, but chases time, to chafe its victim without limit, or calculation of a terminus.

Now there are at this time several direct male descendants of Count Zinzendorff in this country, eminently of sound mind, filling important stations in the Moravian Church, and deservedly popular for their talent, education, and social bearing; perpetuating the self-sacrificing spirit of their great great grandsire, unlet and unmolested by the frantic impetus of the inheritance common to the unfortunate offspring of mental aberration.

CHAPTER III.

Zinzendorff's Hymnology and Poetic Talent—Defence—Qualification.

But for the propriety and the desire to present the original labors of Zinzendorff in America, but more especially in our city, stripped of the stigma of a curiosity of his times, it were less necessary than expedient, to clear my passage to his borders. And so far as we are concerned, Watson's biographical hint, as well as the subject before me, might have slept on the "cooling-board of time."

In pursuance, therefore, of duty, justice, and propriety, I take occasion further to note an ingenuous objection in the twelfth volume of "Chambers's Repository;" which, after a lucid and kindly view of the Count and his doings, thus proceeds: "In the older and more objectionable hymns, we find a number puerile, others highly offensive in taste and imagery!" Undeniable as is this truth, it is not beyond controversy, nor obnoxious to defence or palliation.

The eccentricity of Zinzendorff is conceded; and was especially apparent in his colloquial and idiomatic manner of venting his conceptions.

His imagination was vivid, susceptible, and rapid; whilst the warmth of his temperament, imbued with childlike simplicity, embodied and gave wings to the ardor of his zeal; and the obstacle of poetic refinement was merged in the more facile current of poetical license. Hence, the puerility of his imagery was, doubtless, adapted to that of his babes in Christ, with whom he had constant intercourse, and to whom he spoke, professionally and socially, in terms and similies most familiar to their understanding. Much of which, however adapted to his times and purposes, must appear crude in ours, after the polish of a hundred years of even the mode of thinking.

The strength of some other of his imagery, though couched offensively to our ears, was certainly not so to the hearers of *his* times, any more than was the very extravagant terms of the fourth song of Solomon to the translators and compilers of the Old Testament. Enthusiasm appears to have elasticised their imagination, and their conceptions reflected the impress in bold and unfledged imagery.

His poetic genius, notwithstanding, was rich, apt, and forcible.

Latrobe, in his preface to his Life, says, "As a hymnologist, he claims a distinguished rank in Germany." Again, "They"—his hymns—"are, as might be expected, of unequal merit, are pervaded by the spirit of genuine poetry." "So fertile was his genius, and so ready his power of versification, that he not unfrequently composed and gave out extemporaneous hymns, which were sung by the church in his house, or by the congregation assembled on festal occasions."

Testimony of his poetic genius is not necessary. But the reference above is offered to show that the puerility on the one hand, and the offensiveness on the other, of some of his hymnology, were the pure offerings of a grateful heart, consecrated to the service of his Lord and Master, and by no means the evaporation of a diseased head.

Willing to admit the whims, oddities, and imperfections of Zinzendorff, we feel and know that they can all be compassed in the bands of charitable conclusions.

Eccentricities are often spasmodic, but not the less sane and sound in their issues; but the results of the labors of such a one ought to be forever a passport of their memory to generations to come.

In the case of our patron, we can give him the fruits of his hands, and let his own works praise him in the gates, and thus present him shining through the clouds of obloquy, and lighting up the path of his opening to the succession of his spiritual administration.

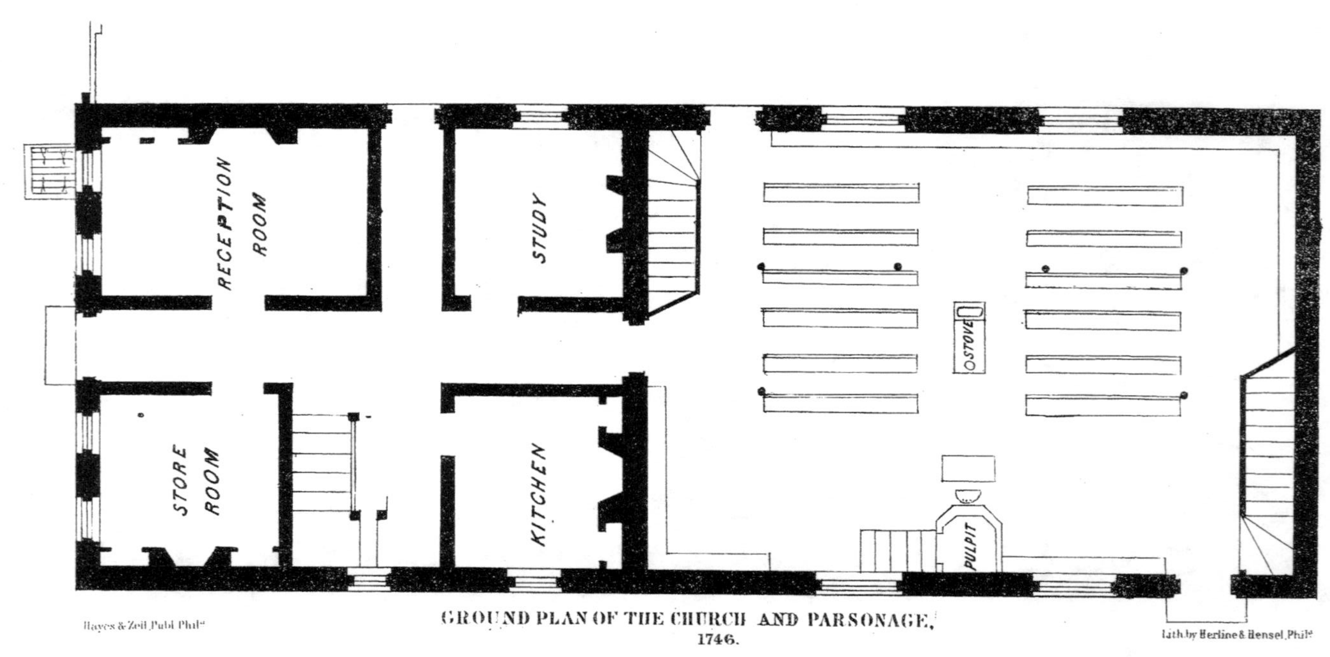

Hayes & Zell Publ Phil^a

GROUND PLAN OF THE CHURCH AND PARSONAGE,
1746.

Lith. by Herline & Hensel, Phil^a

CHAPTER IV.

The Location of the first Moravian Church—Title, &c.

In pursuance of his object to establish a church and congregation, and in conformity with the earnest desire of those converted under his ministry, he selected and took up a lot of ground, at the southeast corner of an avenue, between Second and Third Streets, running south to Arch Street, of thirty-five feet on Race Street, by one hundred and two feet on the avenue or alley.

This avenue took the name of Moravian Alley, and was so recognized until the march of improvement, that so veraciously feeds on ancient landmarks, thought well to refine it to Bread Street, why or wherefore, it would be hard to tell; it was, however, a whim of our city fathers, who a few years ago did so alter and amend the names and finger-boards of all our lanes, streets, and alleys, that our citizens became not only strangers in their own city, but strangers were misled and confused as to their earlier knowledge of the facilities of Philadelphia for former regularity.

The lot above mentioned was secured and appropriated about the middle of the year 1742, but the regular deed did not pass, and was not executed till August 20th, 1743. Whatever may have been the cause of this suspension of formal or legal transfer, history or tradition does not say;

certain, however, it is, that the title did then pass, and was vested as follows:

DEED, AUGUST 20, 1743.

William Allen and wife, to Samuel Powell, Joseph Powell, Edward Evans, William Rice, John Okley, and Owen Rice, for thirty-five feet of ground, east and west, on Sassafras Street, by one hundred and two feet deep, which Andrew Hamilton, the father of Margaret, wife of William Allen, by his will, 31st of July, 1741, devised to his said daughter, Reddendum to the said William Allen and wife, her heirs and assigns, for the yearly rent of *5l. 5s.* sterling, from the 16th November, yearly, forever.

This was of course a trust, by common consent, but not declared till 1746, when the following Declaration of Trust was made by the above Samuel Powell, et alia, as follows:

DECLARATION OF TRUST, APRIL 22, 1746.

Declaring the use to be vested in a certain congregation of Christian people, as well German as English, residing in the city of Philadelphia, belonging to the Church of the Evangelic Brethren, who had caused to be erected thereon a new building, for and then in their use and service, and intended so to be and remain in their use and service, for and as a church and school-house, to S. Lewis, Thurnstein Knight, David Nitchman, Joseph Spangenberg, Henry Antes, John Broomfield, and Charles Brockden.

DEED, AUGUST 20, 1761.

Joseph Spangenberg, et alia, conveys to Peter Bohler,

Nathaniel Seidel, Gottlieb Petzold, Frederick Marshall, and Timothy Horsefield, all the above lot, together with the church and parsonage then completed.

Thus far the Society had been confined to the above thirty-five feet, but subsequently they purchased the lot adjoining on the east, twenty-five feet front on Race Street, more or less. Title derived as follows:

DEED, JANUARY 2, 1739–40.

James Parrock to Lawrence Kunze, twenty-five feet on Race Street, by one hundred and two feet deep, on ground-rent of 3*l.* 16*s.* 6*d.* per annum.

Kunze died intestate, and the lot was afterwards sold and conveyed as follows:

DEED, JANUARY 15, 1782.

Jacob von Reid and Margaret his wife, Henry Winnemore, Jacob Clein and Mary his wife, and Conrad Ort and Mary his wife, heirs of Lawrence Kunze, to John Cornman, Godfrey Hager, Conrad Gerhard, Adam Goos, George Schlosser, and John Peter. Consideration, 500*l.* Pennsylvania currency.

Although these lots were separately conveyed, their interest and purpose was one, and they finally became so in form as well as in fact. The succession of trusts, however, continue until December 25th, 1851, when it was vested in the "Elders of the First Moravian Church of Philadelphia," by John Warner and Thomas C. Lueders, the last surviving trustees of the succession.

Against the ancient possession of this lot, the Church

proper, dignified by time, yet but a mote to the eye of Dame Capricio, the fatal march of improvement presented, urged, and enforced its claims,—a privilege purely American; but the memento of the venerable Zinzendorff was to be scattered to the winds.

Admitting the incapacity of the edifice for an increasing congregation, there was wealth enough in the church to preserve this ancient landmark, and locate elsewhere and more eligibly. The question was agitated, but subdued by the very power that should have cast its influence in the scale of protection.

Again there was a proposition to do what has recently been done, to sell this, however—which would have been as bad and perhaps worse than what was done—and build, either in the centre or on the edge of the Burial-Ground, on Vine Street; but the project failed, and in the early part of the year 1819, it was finally and fully determined to pull down, and rebuild on the same old site.

On the 12th of May, 1819, the corner-stone of the new church was laid. But there I must leave it, until its predecessor gives place to its claims; *ad interim*, however, it will not be out of place to introduce, in connection with the earlier dates, the Burial-Ground, with its title and location.

CHAPTER V.

The Burial-Ground—Title—First interments, &c. &c.

The church had no burial-ground of its own, from its date, 1743 to 1757; and it appears, from the church register, which dates from January 1st, 1743, that the dead were interred in various grounds in the city, either by courtesy or contract.

The first entry reads thus: "1744. Mrs. Manny, the wife of —— Manny, of this town, sail-maker, departed this life, September 25th, and was buried in the English Church burying-ground, the day following, aged sixty years."

Second, thus: "Frederick Clemm, a married man, of this town, barber, departed this life, October 14th, and was buried in the Potter's Field, by John Jacob Doehling; aged about thirty years."

"1745. William, the son of William and Rebeka Nixon, departed this life, March, 12th, aged two months; was buried in William Price's lot, near Bedminster, the day following, by Christopher Pyraleus."

"1746. Mary Batson, the daughter of Thomas and Mary Batson, departed this life, January 2d, and was buried, the day following, in Thomas Say's Burying-Ground."

Say's Burying-Ground is situate on Third Street,

west side, between Market and Arch, probably originally on the line of the street; but now bounded on the east by two stores, Nos. 34 and 36; and on the west and north by the Quaker Burying-Ground.

Immediately on the south, adjoining, there was a private burial-ground, located and owned by James Porteus, a bachelor, who lived in the kitchen of the main building, and died, and was buried on his lot, about one hundred and fifty feet from the line of Third Street, whose slab yet marks the spot, and thus records: "Here lays the body of James Porteus, who departed this life, the 19th day of January, 1733, aged seventy-two years."

The above are *verbatim et literatim* copies from the record, and are given as well as specimens of old-time simplicity, as to fill the gap from 1743 to 1757, touching the very important appendage to every church,—a depository for the dead.

This gap is filled by seventy-six recorded deaths. The two last read thus: "Juliana Clay, a widow, went home to our Saviour, 5th of October, '57, and was buried in Kingston—probably Kensington. She lived two miles out of town. She was a friend to us, but not received into our Society."

"Sarah Thorn, wife of William Thorn, went home to our Saviour, October 21st, and was buried in the Quaker Burying-Ground; aged about 30 years."

From 1757 to 1764, there were other deaths and interments out of and from the Mission, principally converted Indians, and a few whites, as heretofore, in different grounds, as, perhaps, opportunity offered, or circumstances required. Of such there were fifty-five, male and female, young and old.

The margin notes: "Indians departed in the Barracks, and at Philadelphia, in the year 1764, and buried in the Potter's Field, in the year 1764; of these, forty-nine were of the above fifty-five."

In 1757, the Society purchased a lot, for burial purposes, thus recorded:

DEED, MAY 10, 1757.

Samuel Jones and Amy his wife, heirs of Joshua Lawrence, to Lewis Cassler, for lot of ground in the Northern Liberties, north side of Vine Street, and west side of a fifty-feet street—since called Lawrence Street—being eighty feet two inches front on Vine Street, by one hundred and forty feet on Lawrence Street; granted by patent of John Penn to Joshua Lawrence, with other ground, February 15th, 1734.

Lewis Cassler subsequently conveyed the above, as follows, in trust.

DEED. BURIAL-GROUND. DECEMBER 28, 1786.

Ludwig Cassler to George Schlosser, John Peter, Adam Goos, John Cornman, Thomas Bartow, Godfrey Hager, and Conrad Gerhard, for lot of ground north side of Vine Street, and west side of a fifty-feet street, called Lawrence Street, in trust. Consideration, 82*l.* 15*s.* Pennsylvania currency, or \$215 33⅓.

Witnesses. Signed, SAMUEL JONES,
L. WEISS, AMY JONES.
PETER MILLER.

Thus far the title of the church property. But, as it would be premature to enter the cemetery and bury the dead, before the ingathering of life, I shall proceed to re-build, review, and present the nucleus of the Moravian Church in Philadelphia, as it was from its cradle, 1742–46, when the parsonage was adjoined; thence to its demolition, in 1819; and then give some account of the interments in the new ground, and set forth Moravians and Moravianism, together with their manners and customs, and everything else that may offer touching that early branch of the Christian Church.

THE ORIGINAL MORAVIAN CHURCH OF 1742.

S.E. Corner of Moravian Alley (Now Bread St.) & Race St.

CHAPTER VI.

Location and Description of the Exterior—East and West Fronts of the Church Edifice, and View of the Church Edifice—Eastern Front without the Parsonage.

As stated above, the lot was the southeast corner of Race Street, and a twenty feet passage or avenue to Arch Street, probably nameless before the Church suggested the designation of "Moravian Alley."

Its dimensions were thirty-five feet on Race Street, by one hundred and two on the avenue.

Foresight, economy, and expediency, as well as inability, suggested the propriety of reserving sufficient depth on Race Street for the very important appendage, when circumstances should warrant, of a parsonage, or, more properly, a "Mission House," so called, because of its intended purposes of accommodating the Brethren of the Mission, of and belonging to this station, besides others of this "household of faith."

The church building was, therefore, set back about thirty-five feet from the line of Race Street. Its dimensions were, taking the fronts on Race Street, thirty feet by about forty-five feet on Moravian Alley.

The sexes being separated in their sittings, two fronts were necessary for their respective entrance, and hence, five feet on the east was reserved and kept open for a passage to the entrance of that front. The building was about twenty feet in height to the eaves, from which started the broken pitch or hip-roof, about ten feet to the peak or upper ridge, the object of which I shall presently show.

At the extreme south of the western front, was the sisters' door; whilst on the extreme north of the eastern front, was that of the brethren.

Two windows on the east, and two directly opposite on the west, were the apertures for light and air; besides a small upper window on the extreme south of the eastern front, to serve the gallery and its occupants with like comfort and convenience.

The four main windows started full six feet from the ground, but stretched up thence to very near the eaves.

There was no fancy about these conveniences. Windows and doors were entirely unpretending in their offerings. Glass, nine by eleven, and plain square-framed doors, about three feet six inches by six feet six inches, were dignified by their office or purpose, and gave tone to the humble conceptions of their architect.

The walls were of good hard brick, not pressed front stretchers, but hard brick, interspersed with glazed black-headers, showing their object of breaking the monotonous red. Some very old buildings, yet in being, tell of this variety and taste of the olden time.

The annexed plate is as near a fac simile as memory, grafted in the susceptible prime of youth, can delineate; and this, I am happy to say, is fully confirmed by several surviving contemporaries of these times. Not, however, of 1742, but of 1798, and onward during the existence of the building.

The eastern front was but a reflection of the western; but, for reasons first given, it was a corresponding front.

Of this edifice, the corner-stone was laid on the 10th day of September, 1742, and the rapidity of the workmen rendered it available for consecration, which ceremony was performed by Count Zinzendorff, on the 25th day of November following.

Rapid as was this work, it was well and substantially done; it had neither break nor crack in its walls, in any part of the building.*

The congregation, as such, was not yet formed; but the spiritual gatherings of the Count, desirous of a closer communion with the Unity of the Brethren, he, according to their wish, constituted his thirty-four members into a Moravian congregation, on New Year's day of the year 1743.

On the 30th of June, 1746, this congregation commenced the addition of a parsonage, or congregation-house, extending their borders on the east, by the lot of twenty-five feet, purchased of the heirs of Lawrence Kunze; which lot or conveyance, must have been held *in escrow* from 1739–40 to 1746.

The addition of this building, and the adjoining lot, gave finish, dignity, and character to the whole.

* In the latter part of the last century, the building was struck by lightning, which cracked the east wall of the parsonage, after shattering a bedstead in one of the chambers, but no one was hurt. A lightning-rod was planted, and run up to the chimney-top of the parsonage, immediately after this accident.

CHAPTER VII.

The Parsonage—Interior Arrangements—Purposes—Minister's Support.

THE dimensions of this building were thirty feet front, by thirty-five deep; it was two and a half stories in height to the apex, the broken pitch conforming exactly with that of the church proper.

There were four rooms on the first floor, divided north and south by a passage from the front door to the entrance of the church, by a small doorway, inserted for the accommodation of the minister; on the west, by a wide, open stairway; and directly opposite by a passage eastward to the yard.

The northeast room was the minister's parlor, or reception-room, about twelve by fifteen feet in size; of humble garniture, consisting of a ten-plate stove, plain small mahogany table, a small mahogany looking-glass, in the pier, a rag carpet, and a few Windsor chairs, an old-fashioned shelf, high above the fireplace, over which strode the stove-pipe to its entrance into the chimney.

The southeast room was the study and private apartment of the minister, furnished with a table, a few chairs, rag carpet, and a small stove. The southwest apartment was the kitchen, and the northwest was variously used, as necessity or expediency required, for domestic purposes.

Hayes & Zell P d. Phila

Lith. by Herline & Hensel, Phila

THE ORIGINAL MORAVIAN CHURCH OF 1746 TO 1820 WITH THE PARSONAGE,

S.E. Corner of Moravian Alley (Now Race St) & Race St.

The stairway was guarded by a broad oaken hand-rail, supported by flat fancy banisters; they were commodious in width, and very easy of ascent, being designed for congregational as well as domestic purposes; lit by day, by a window over the first landing, and by night, by a taper floating upon an inch depth of oil, in a plain glass globe, suspended at the corner of the passage leading into the yard, whose glimmer served fairly the fourfold purpose of lighting up the points of the compass.

There was no waste of oil or tallow in those days. Small favors were respectfully appreciated, and thankfully appropriated. Our fathers used their blessings, comforts, and conveniences as not abusing them.

The second floor was divided into five or six small sleeping apartments, as was, likewise, the dormitory, excepting a passage in the latter, from the stairway to the upper audience chamber of the church, into which a doorway had been inserted as below; of all which in their proper order.

This building was planned and arranged not only for the parsonage of a single resident minister, but for the accommodation of the several missionaries, who were engaged in and about the city, as well also for visiting ministers from the several congregational places established by the Count, and subsequent growth of his early designs; but besides these, it was the welcome of any brother, minister, or man, who might come to the city on business or pleasure; which custom continued into the present century. They were entertained free of cost, frugally, but kindly and comfortably.

There was, at this time, no fixed amount for the support of the clergy; they were cared for by their flocks, as need required; they were called laborers, and as such, were counted worthy of their hire; but the congregation being very small, and certainly not wealthy, its offerings were, of necessity, also small; but still, though they had little, they had no lack, and they were content with such things as they had.

Hayes & Zell, Publ. Phila.

INTERIOR OF THE LOWER AUDIENCE CHAMBER OF THE MORAVIAN CHURCH, OF 1742.

Lith. by Herline & Hensel, Phila.

CHAPTER VIII.

The Lower Audience Chamber of the Church Proper (see drawing annexed)—Organs—Organists and Organ Builders.

THE lower audience chamber was thirty feet wide, by about forty-five feet in length on Moravian Alley. Its height was about twenty feet from the floor. The walls were wainscoted to the height of about five feet; above which were the plain whitewashed walls, to the ceiling, which was also whitewashed.

On the southern end, an old-fashioned, broad, hand-rail, flat banister, enclosed an easy flight of stairs, to a landing, two-thirds of the way up, starting from near the women's door, and turning to the gallery; and there was a corresponding flight from the men's door on the northern end. Each of these stairways was guarded by a gate below, with a bolt on it, but besides, were protected from unbidden or foreign material by a *chapel servant.** Boys and girls were generally required to stay below. On the west side, between the windows, stood an old-time, pedestal, ogee pulpit, with five or six risers, or steps, to its entrance and seat, which was a board inserted in the wall, *sans arms or cushion.* The desk for the Bible, too, was an uncushioned board, extending some six inches over the pulpit's edge.

* *Chapel servant,* the early term for sexton; called in German, *Diener.*

In front, directly over the bulge of the pulpit, was a large gloria of wood, of coarsely carved rays, darting irregularly from a dark centre, which held the letters I. H. S. The rays and letters were gilt.

Previous to the year 1805, this pulpit had no sounding-board; in that year, however, Joseph Worrel, a carpenter, and a member of the church, made, presented, and affixed this appendage in the wall, a very short way above the minister's head; it was neither round nor elliptic, but five-sided.

In front of this pulpit, there was a square oaken table, covered with plain green ratinet, behind which stood an old-fashioned, high, cane-back, but rush-bottomed chair, now in good preservation, and in the possession of John Jordan, Jun'r, whence came the catechetical authority to the doubting, timid urchin, as he awaited his turn to answer some unanticipated question.

The area of this chamber was furnished with some twenty benches, of ten feet in length, ten for each sex, leaving an aisle, east and west, of about six or eight feet.

These benches had top-rails and arms, stained and polished, but no other back than the top-rail.

In front of these were, at each side, one of lower order, for boys and girls, catechumens under twelve years of age,—who, although yet catechumens, were promoted to the next bench behind, after they had attained their twelfth year.

Antecedent to the year 1794, the aisle just described was cleai of all incumbrance ; and it would appear, from the following minute, that up to that time no provision whatever was made for warming the church. The minute reads thus:

"Oct. 12, 1794. Agreed, that a ten-plate stove in our church be purchased; and that the Brethren Hager and Smallwood, have the charge thereof."

In December, same year, the purchase was reported to the "Standing Committee of the Church," as follows:

1 ten-plate stove, ...	£3	15	0
Furnishing the same, ...	2	12	6
42 feet of pipe, at 19*d*., ...	3	6	6
1 cord of wood; hauling and sawing, . .	3	10	7
	£13	4	7
Abated on account, ...		2	0
	£13	2	7

Or, $35 and a fraction.

This stove was placed in the centre of the aisle; and, as the church had no chimneys, the pipe, elevated to the gallery girder, passed under it and out of the eastern window, into the yard; whilst fuel, shovel, and tongs, were all snugly arranged beneath the stove, ready to serve any well-wisher to the comforts of their brethren and sisters. The warming, therefore, of the Moravian Church, in Philadelphia, commenced late in the fall of the year 1794.

But, to return to my description. Along the wainscoting, except the space occupied by the pulpit and stairs, a plain bench offered its services to any one not else seated. An entrance having been made from the parsonage into the church, in the centre of the north wall, immediately behind the staircase, the chapel servant, for the time being, always sat at the end of that wall-bench leading to this door, whose business it was to call and wait on the minister into the church, and shut the door after him, at the proper time of commencing service, and open the door again as he left the pulpit.

The two western windows were curtained, to break the glare of the afternoon sun, by long streamers of green ratinet, hung on an iron rod at the top by small rings, and drawn right and left by a cord, extending in a graceful curve below the window-sill, and within reach of the proper operator. These windows, being high from the floor, could not be reached nor raised, except from the full elevation of the bench below; and, even then, the tiptoe was called to do its part.

The north and south galleries were furnished with plain box-seats, without any backs, except a strip of two or three inches, rising from the seat. Of these, there were two rows, besides the wall seats, all or any of which were seldom occupied till 1817; the ground floor, till then, being sufficient for all the comforts and conveniences of the congregation.

In the centre of the eastern gallery, directly opposite to the pulpit, stood a small organ, of five stops, with gilt pipes in front, and broken scroll cornice, with a small gilt eagle, with extended wings, peering upon the organist from the pedestal between the scrolls.

The dignified appearance of the organ was considerably enhanced by side-panels, extending its breadth about two feet on each side, ornamented with an oval of gilt show-pipes. The disposition of the instrument was as follows:

1. Stop, d Diapason.
2. Open do.
3. Flute.
4. Principal.
5. Fifteenth.

The metallic tones of the latter flew richly through the diapasons, and gave brilliancy to the whole. It was a spirited affair, and yet sufficiently subdued for the more solemn service in its diapasons alone.

It appears, from the minutes of November, 1796, that this organ had a predecessor, which, being declared old, and in a state of decay, was ordered to be sold, and another procured.

In May, 1797, the committee heretofore appointed to carry out this project, report, "that they have sold the organ to the steward of the 'Union Church, at White Hall, Northampton County,' at the price of 50*l.* (a pretty good sale), and that they had purchased a new organ, of Peter Kurtz (the organist then, and for many years after, of Christ Church), for 105*l.*; and, in November, 1797, paid David Dannenberg (Tannenberg), 11*s.* 6*d.* (eleven shillings and sixpence), for extra tuning."*

* Peter Kurtz died on the 12th of April, 1816, and was buried in Christ Church Ground, southeast corner of Fifth and Arch Streets.

This veteran organist was the *capelle meister* of Christ Church, for upwards of forty years; and, when seated at the foot of his instrument, looked as though he had grown in the seat. He was of the old German school; his voluntaries, preludes, and interludes, though just and true, were strictly editions of each other; fancy, to him, was yet unborn, except so far as the north and south running and rolling over the scale, was so considered; and he enjoyed his post, too, saving the dereliction of Jerry, the colored bellows-blower, who sometimes forgot that it took two to make the music,—when Jerry, at the top of the organ, and Kurtz below, would exchange sharps in whispers, but severe in purpose. The bellows of this organ was situated at the back of the top, whence, the wind was conveyed by "trunks" to the "chest" below. Jerry was therefore exalted, and could smile at his master below, with impunity.

Tannenberg belongs to history as *the* organ builder of his day, and one of renown. He, too, was of the German school. Fancy stops were not

How long before 1787 the old organ gave tone to and from that spot, data saith not; but in that year, it certainly was there, seeing that the organist was reproved by the Committee of the Church, for bad or improper playing, and the organ closed, for a season, against his determined disobedience, then and there.

Though a mere epitome of an organ, it was supplied by two unusually large bellows, on the south side, not less than three feet wide by six feet long each, and with one fold; they were set in a frame, one above the other, upon the cross-beams of which rested, in a fulcrum, a long heavy lever to each, which required some strength to bring down from its angular quiet. This was the honorable post of your author, though a mere stripling, whose main strength was enhanced by the pleasurable anticipation of an *ad interim* seat at the southeast window, overshadowed by a fruitful peach tree, and the chance of an occasional relish, as the good old minister turned his head and his attention from this garden of Eden.

The north side of this gallery was open to the choir exclusively, which consisted of some four or five boys, of which I, too, was one, when particular occasions called for extra services in that department, at which time we were seated either on a backless bench there, or on a like

generally in vogue, except the trumpet in the great organ, and the vox humana in the swell, of which latter, there was but one in the city, and that was in Christ Church; and to my young ear, a good imitation of the human voice.

There are several of Tannenberg's organs yet in breathing existence. Lancaster, Litiz, and Nazareth still hold his memory in audible and respectful tones; and much of his work is worthy of imitation. His diapasons were particularly dignified, whilst his upper work, 12th, 15th, and sesquialtera, gave brilliancy to the whole.

accommodation between the bellows and the front of the gallery; in such cases, being promoted for the time being, a substitute manned the bellows' pole.

It may be remarked here, that the musical department of the church was of the most sacred regard, and that the hymning of religious sentiment was tested by the sincerity of the offering. Prayer, praise, supplication, and thanksgiving, being concentrated into rhythmic beauty, and uttered in tones melodious, were not the less worship for their mode of offering; of which, however, more in the sequel.

It will be also in place to state here, that the organ first described was sold to John Shermer, a watchmaker, resident in North Second Street, near Coates, west side, in exchange for a new one of four stops, built by him; valuing the old one at $120, and his at $400, paying, therefore, the difference of $280,—all which was completed, and the new organ up in the church on the 10th of February, 1809.

The objections to the old organ do not appear; but although Shermer's genius spoke well for its source, except the bulk and place required for the bellows,—there was not much gained by the exchange.

The arrangement for lighting this chamber for evening service, though simple, was not without some dignity, since, beside the tin candle-holders, hung here and there on the several posts, under the gallery, a brass sconce hung imposingly from the centre of the ceiling to within about six feet from the floor. The body of this sconce—its proper name in those days—was a bulb of about ten inches in diameter, presenting six graceful curved branches, from a band and sockets around its centre, having a knob below by which to draw it from, or return it to, its equilibrium.

The evening service being seldom held from the pulpit, the lights there were temporary.

The table below, being mostly used by the minister for these services, was supplied, as occasion required, by two clever-sized tallow candles, subsequently substituted by spermaceti, as refinement pressed its claims.

The annexed drawing shows the principal half of this area and its fixtures, to which I confidently refer, and pass on to the upper chamber, which, in reality, was the most important, being kept exclusively for all private meetings, to wit, receptions, confirmations, communions, love-feasts, &c. &c.; and was, therefore, in fact, the starting-point or nucleus of the congregation.

CHAPTER IX.

Description of the Hall—Upper Chamber—Use of, &c.

THE upper chamber was called "The Hall," and was reached by a close, narrow stairway, from the southern gallery, and entered by the brethren by a small door, at the head of this short flight of stairs, and by the sisters, through an entrance from the attic of the parsonage.

Its dimensions were the same as the floor below, and its floor was supported by a heavy girder, extending the whole length, from north to south, of the church edifice, resting on the north and south walls, forty-five feet apart; yet as firm as a rock.

This girder was subsequently used, being slit longitudinally, as girders for the gallery of the immediate successor to this ancient pile; and although, eighty years in service, as a support to the gathering above, and a reflector or sounding-board to that below, was unscathed in every part, and sound from centre to circumference.

The arrangement of the benches here, was the same as that below, as well in the general area as along the walls.

The walls were wainscoted from the floor to the ceiling inclusive, and in form followed the rafters, leaving, however, a flat surface of some five or six feet, to square off the apex of the roof.

Daylight here was neither strong nor extensive. There

were three dormer windows on the east and three on the west side, and a square window in the south gable end, at the head of the stairs; one of these dormer windows at each side of this attic, opened midway into this area, and from the pitch of the room formed a sort of recess.

The minister's table and chair, somewhat better finished than the same below, was placed immediately under the easternmost window, having the sisters on the right, and the brethren on the left.

In the southeast corner stood the organ, a sweet little affair of three stops, facing north. This was the musical department, and was guarded by a ten-feet bench, upon which sat the elder members of the church, as well for their own convenience, as to guard, watch, and keep in order the juvenile choristers, who were privileged thus to sit behind them. This enclosure was exclusive, none but the members of the choir being admitted, and they consisted of the organist and four or six boy singers, the bellows-blower, and an old indispensable, who considered the music very imperfect without the twang of his fiddle, to which he attached more importance than the minister or his audience; of which, however, and the choir music in general, more in its turn.

This hall being mostly used for evening service, and, moreover, a kind of sanctum, was more refined in appearance, and more dignified in character, and although uncarpeted, its milk-white floor and general neat attire were always interesting and inviting. The floor below was sanded; this was not.

The chandelier (sconce) was the issue of good taste. The body was elongated, of some fanciful indentations, and four medium fancy branches for candles; this, suspended from the ceiling, was run up and down, as the one below, and gave considerable dignity to the place of its abode. In addition to this, two tall brass candlesticks, with extra-sized candles, on the minister's table, and two boldly curved branches, one from each cheek of the window, over or rather behind him, illuminated the great centre; whilst two or three candles about the organ, and as many more at the opposite end, in tin candle-holders, distributed light in all required abundance; of all which the annexed drawing is a graphic description. But whilst we could boast of plenty of light, and that, too, in jets from fancy's offering, we could not dilate upon the abundance of heat, or even moderate warmth. There was no arrangement for this comfort, and the only medium of heat, to qualify the air, or chafe the chill of this chamber, was borrowed from below; to which end, some hours in advance of meetings to be held above, a smart fire was made, kept up in the stove below, and the door at the head of the stairs being left open, the generating redundance of the stove sought refuge as far above as it could get—a sensible alternative, as it was also a sensitive comfort; but not quite enough for the old sisters, whose happy medium, always *au fait*, brought forth their *foot-stoves*, with porringer of live hickory coals, to complete this desideratum.

In this sanctum there was, as well as below, some differences in the sittings, but without distinction. The younger part of the congregation not being admitted, the front benches were occupied by the elders on one side, and their wives on the other; whilst, most prominent of all, sat the chapel servant, under the eave, on a wall-bench, some three feet only from the side of the minister, with snuffers at hand to clip and remove the darksome refuse of heat and tallow.

This hall was not painted till June, 1791, when it was done by Jabez Emory.

THE USE OF THE HALL.

As before stated, this hall was kept for and used only on special occasions, for private meetings, and the more sacred ordinances of the church, viz.:

The "washing of feet," in pursuance of the example of our Saviour.

The Holy Communion, in obedience to his command.

The love-feasts, in continuance of the early custom of the Christian Church, for its harmonizing influence upon the congregation.

The reception of members into the congregation. And,

The ejection of obstinate backsliders, or immoral members, who would neither "hear, nor forbear."

In every case of a meeting here, the brethren of the congregation gathered first, and sat in order below, and at the appointed time—and they were exact to a minute—the chapel servant came from the hall to the gallery's edge, and beckoned with his hand, when all rose and went up, "decently and in order;" and when they were seated, the sisters came in from the attic of the parsonage—in the earlier times *without* bonnets, but in plain caps. Meanwhile, the organist was solemnizing the assemblage by a befitting voluntary.

The original entrance to the hall for the sisters, was by a corresponding flight of stairs from the gallery to the one on the south end, already noted; but after the connection of the parsonage, they passed up by the stairway of its entry,—also heretofore set forth,—to the antechambers in the attic, where they prepared for their call to the service.

CHAPTER X.

Front Entrance—Gardens, &c., of and to the Church and Parsonage.

PRIOR to the year 1746, the entrance to the church, on the eastern front, was evidently only by a five-feet passage, because the actual width of the foundation on Race Street, recently measured,* not having been disturbed by the modern improvements, is exactly thirty feet, which also determined the exact depth of the church.

Subsequently, being in full possession of the lot adjoining on the east, and the parsonage being built, five feet was added to the passage, and gave a ten-feet opening to the church, as well as a passage to a neatly cultivated garden on the rear of the church premises, and a reserved part of the eastern addition.

Besides the varied cultivation of this reservation with fruits and flowers, and very plenty of the latter, there was a vastly prolific peach tree in the passage, whose waving branches so often and so opportunely paid their respects at my window, with its grateful and irresistible offerings.

On the front of this lot there was a two-story frame, which was alternately occupied as a store, storehouse, and finally a cabinet-maker shop and wareroom, at a rent varying from 50*l.* to 15*l.*, and raising again to 30*l.* per annum;

* The original foundation being yet in its place.

reserving about forty feet of the rear end, to enlarge the garden at the rear and side of the church.

There was also a small frame tenement on the southern end of the church lot, on Moravian Alley, occupied for many years as a turner-shop, by John Stow, at 14*l.* per annum.

The garden here spoken of was one of no mean appearance.

Our good old rector, Brother John Meder, was as indefatigable in his secular duties, as he was earnest in his labors of love. He lost no time, but ever and anon caught the fleeting moment, and planted it in his garden, or marked its flight by a more imperious call.

The garden, therefore, sharing his industry, was also redolent of his taste and skill, and the privileged turn within its enclosure was fully enjoyed, not only with its sweetly-scented atmosphere, but by the liberal permission to dress the button-hole with a sprig or blossom, that needs must yield to the covetous eye or curious touch of a wistful wanderer over its paths.

Roses various, lilacs, heart's-ease, lilies, &c.; peach, pear, and plum trees, were hailed by aerial songsters above; whilst the sward below sent forth the untiring trill of the flirty and bounding grasshopper, whose serenade never gave place to time or circumstances, but was rather intrusive upon the more tender tones of the minister.

In these presentations of the early history of this church, there is necessarily a mixture of recollections; but, be assured, reader, that these recollections are in no wise flowers of fancy; they were planted in the early soil of my existence, and their garden has only grown in verdure, to create an oasis in the desert of declining life.

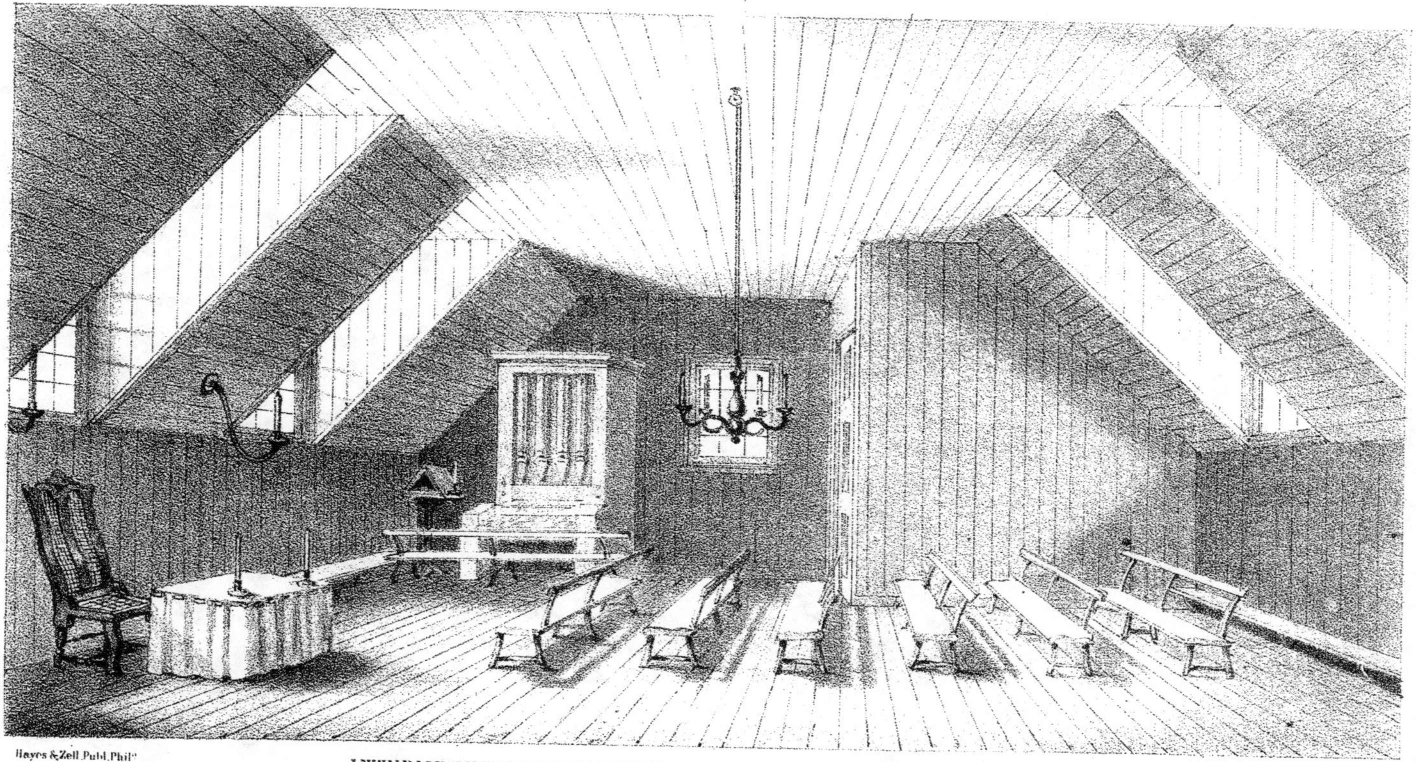

Hayes & Zell Publ. Phil^a

Lith. by Herline & Hensel Phil^a

INTERIOR OF THE UPPER CHAMBER OR HALL OF THE MORAVIAN CHURCH,
OF 1742.

Data must be my authority; and to data I appeal to gather up the fragments that constitute the history of our ecclesiological existence, and the venerable tabernacle that gathered, nursed, and furthered the pioneers of this portion of the Christian Church in America.

Hence, then, I must return to the place of beginning; show up the nucleus, and bring up the congregation, as time and the grace of God increased their spiritual and their temporal strength.

CHAPTER XI.

The Primitive Opening of the Church—Organization—Original Officers and Succession, &c.

THE original object of Count Zinzendorff was not sectarian, but a general exercise of Christian benevolence; gathering up from any and every quarter within his reach, his scattered and neglected German brethren.

The thirty-four persons that constituted his congregation in Philadelphia, were, of course, close adherents to his principles and doctrine, and became willing subjects of his discipline. His ecclesiastical associates were nearly as numerous as his lay members; but his missionary compass naturally rendered his and their duties itinerant; and wherever he or they could obtain an audience, large or small, there they sowed the seed of spiritual life. The sphere of their labors being thus extensive, but transient—the Count himself being here but for a very short time, and all that time variously and unintermittingly engaged—there were no regular minutes kept of their proceedings, except memoranda on loose leaves, some of which have been spared the ruthless tooth of time, and present their gatherings for the information of our day.

From this we gather the following succession of the ministry, from 1743 to 1785; the latter being the date of regular minutes.

1741. Count Nicholas Louis de Zinzendorff, having established his head-quarters at Bethlehem, in this State, gave freedom to his sacerdotal services, alternately here, as well as there, and in other places, from his advent to his departure for Europe; during which time, John Christoper Pyrlaeus appears to have been his more immediate associate in the ministry here, and afterwards, with others, succeeded him, and continued the work in Bethlehem.

Peter Boehler, an active, eminent, and effectual fellow-worker in the Gospel; David Bruce, Thomas Yarrel, —— Okely, Owen Rice, Richard Utley, —— Evans, Thomas Greening, Matthew Reitz, Richard Bonner, Andrew Eschenbach, John Bechtel, and Daniel Neubert, were all engaged in the itinerancy, and were contemporaries from 1743 to 1747.

These brethren, though noted as associated in the spread of the Gospel in and about Philadelphia, were not confined to its limits; but we find some of them laboring alternately in this period, in New York, where a sister society had been formed in 1740, under the pastorate of Peter Boehler, who, after his efforts in Georgia, came on to that colony.

I cannot help remarking here that this very Peter Boehler was the bosom friend and co-worker with the Count, at and before the time, 1740–43, that Logan writes, and Watson unqualifiedly quotes him as "a mere knight-errant in religion," and "as scarcely less than Don Quixote in chivalry." And this very Peter Boehler, whom Wesley, the founder of one of the most useful, energetic, evangelical, and extensive denominations of Christians in the world, the Methodists, acknowledges as his spiritual father. A most awful infliction of unlimited insanity, if Logan's wisdom were exemplified at the present day.

But to the succession.

From 1747 to 1751. Abraham Reinke,
Owen Rice, and
John Gambold,

were associate ministers, with the exception of Abraham Reinke, who being called, or sent elsewhere, was substituted by Richard Utley. 1751 to 1753, Brother Reinke is again in his place, and thence to 1754, we have the Brethren Herman, Jacob Rogers, John Brandtmiller, Abra. L. Rusmayer.

1754 to 1756. John Valentine Haidt,
Christopher Frank, and again,
Thomas Yarrel.

1756 to 1762.

Christian Otto Krogstrup, Jasper Payne, —— Herman, Jacob Rogers, —— Till, Henry Beck.

1762 to 1774.

George Neissor, Richard Utley again, and Jacob Fries.

1774 to 1784.

Daniel Sydrick alone had charge of the congregation, subject to visits and aid from the authorities at Bethlehem, which he also obtained and perhaps needed in this still infancy of the church.

Transient visits had been made before by the brethren, Bishop Spangenberg, Frederick Cammerhoff, George Soelle, and services rendered, but the regular succession appears to have been as above, the last of which was the return of George Neissor, in 1784, latter part of the year, who died on the 1st of November, of that year, and is amongst the early tenants of the silent congregation of Vine and Franklin Streets.

The itinerancy of the mission seems to have ended here. The congregation being settled, the several ministers, heretofore necessary to supply this church and its various outposts, were withdrawn to supply other stations, intermediately formed and established, by the Count and his assistants in the ministry.

Bethlehem being the head-quarters of the Church at large, and the seat of government, laws, rules, orders, and regulations, were issued thence, and was as well the receptacle—obligato—of reports of the temporal and spiritual doings of the branches of its Church.

Hence during the forty-two years of itinerancy here, the authorities there were kept alive to the doings of their brethren, and their protocol was supplied by reports of the progress of the mission here. Whilst here, only memoranda on loose sheets were kept, some of which are yet extant in the archives of the Church in Philadelphia.

The Church being therefore fairly and fully established, the Rev. John de Watteville, son-in-law of the Count, the husband of his eldest daughter, Henrietta Benigna Justina, presented himself as patron to regulate and symplify a more tenable organization of the Church and congregation.

CHAPTER XII.

The Authorities of the Church—Their Source, Order, &c.

In immediate connection with the organization and furtherance of the Church in Philadelphia, it will be important to the chain of my history, to introduce the source and the regulating or governing powers of the churches in America.

Although Count Zinzendorff came to this New World to seek and ameliorate the spiritual condition of his German brethren in general, but at first, labored with and for the Lutherans; yet, as an official, he was a Bishop of the Moravian Church, but came out from thence, divested, for the time, of his robes, and labored as an ordinarius, "becoming all things to all men, so that if by any means, he might win some."

When he, however, established Bethlehem as his headquarters, he made it also the seat of government, and established the authorities there, subject to the parent Church, in Germany, as the higher powers.

The spirit of this authority, and its governing principle, having grown from a monarchial *régime*, claimed the same as a prerogative here, and shed the same influence in all its proceedings, ecclesiastical or secular.

These constituted authorities formed a cabinet, and consisted—

First, of an Administrator, who had charge of the estates belonging to the Church there, and elsewhere, and of the financial department in general, with discretionary power to sell, buy, borrow, or loan, by virtue of his office, the titles of the estates being vested in him personally; and all moneys passing to and fro through him, untrammelled of any security whatever,—except the rendition of his accounts, semi-annually, to the parent authorities in Europe,—in all which the slightest dereliction or *faux pas* with this functionary has never happened; a most wonderful and tenacious faithful continuance in well-doing, but unfortunately not very common in the world.

Secondly. A Conference, styled the "Provincial Helpers' Conference," as subject to that in Europe, called the "Unity's Elders' Conference."

This body consisted of three or five members, from and by whose authority emanated the ecclesiastical charge of the churches; and, although an ecclesiological court of appeal, it was not sufficiently imbued with American liberality, nor, indeed, embossed with republican courtesy, to encourage the privilege, or beckon a hope for a reconsideration, or an amendment of a mandate once gone from its borders. I speak of early times,—1785.

The Bishop, although invested with plenary Episcopal powers, did not exercise lordship over his brethren, nor in any manner exercise the rigor over his Episcopate, excepting only where the prelatical duties of his office required his services, according to the ritual of the Church; for the rest, he acted in common with his brethren in the ministry, subject to their call for counsel or conference.

The Administrator, as well as his colleagues, being all

ordained to minister in holy things, constituted the temporal and spiritual authorities of the Church, from whom issued orders for good manners in their respective settlements, and pastors for the congregations, elsewhere established.

This Conference was governed in all its appointments by the "Lot," an institution in the Church, founded on apostolic example; and, so long as appealed to in untrammelled faith and faithfulness, never erred, and never could err, whilst God is truth and certainty.

But of all this, my history will lead me hereafter to a better and more extensive elucidation.

The authority for proceedings being thus set forth, I appeal to the first regular minutes, to show the beginning, the rise, and the progress of the Moravian Church in Philadelphia.

The Rev. John de Watteville, familiarly called "Brother Johannes," being on a visit from the parent Church in Herrnhuth, to its branches in America, amongst other places, visited the Philadelphia gathering, and organized a local governing power, of which this power thus records.

"Sunday, 5th June, 1785.—The Committee appointed at the visitation of Brother Johannes, to transact the business of the United Brethren's Church, in Philadelphia, met for the first time, viz.:

Bernhardt Adam Grube,
Jacob Fries, } Ministers.

Adam Goose, George Senneff,
George Schlosser, Conrad Gerhardt,
John Peter, Godfrey Haga,
John Cornman, Thomas Bartow, } Standing Committee."

This was considered and called the "Standing Committee;" and for many years, vacancies by death or resignation were filled by themselves.

Of this body, Thomas Bartow was appointed secretary, and general accountant of the Church.

The name of Brother Fries does not appear after this meeting; and Brother Grube also retires between the months of July and October of this year, and Brother John Meder succeeds them in the pastorate.

CHAPTER XIII.

The Finances of the Church.

THE finances of the church were not only small, but slow; and the minister's support was not very luxurious. There was a sustentation account and fund, supplied by voluntary contribution; but the paucity and uncertainty of the supply, induced the committee to form a more reliable compact, which they did by obtaining regular subscriptions of 20*s*. per share, per annum; this, with the small income from the frame shops on the east and south of the premises, enabled them to support the minister, and keep the church and adjoining property in order; but, as yet, there was no fixed amount allotted to the minister.

If the general fund fell short, which it did sometimes, the amount was forthwith raised by private subscription, which, however, always fell on the willing few; and if anything was over, which sometimes also happened by the gathering up of the arrearages, such overplus was handed over to the minister as a present!

But as a missionary station, the congregation was bound to support the minister and his family; to wit, in food, raiment, light, and heat. The parsonage being there for the purpose, of course gave him house rent free.

In 1788, there was a deficit of 16*l.* 4*s.*,* which was at once made up by a few of the more able members, and the account squared.

In 1795, a surplus of 6*l.* 5*s.* was presented to the minister.

The abundance of money was not the kind of wealth that the church required. There were no artificial wants, and no indulgences in luxury of any sort; the income was therefore generally made to fill the vacuum of expenditure; which, with economy and frugality hand in hand, encircled, and kept inordinate desires within bounds.

Church collections were seldom resorted to. There was one annually, for the poor, yielding from 8*l.* to 10*l.*; and one for the Society for the Propagation of the Gospel among the Heathen, commonly called the "Heathen Society," averaging about 13*l.* per annum; but there were no regular Sunday collections. There was a box fixed on the inner side of half the door of egress, on the men's and the women's side, to receive the voluntary droppings of the retiring congregation.

The special collections were taken at each door, on a pewter plate, held by the chapel servant.

A rather ludicrous circumstance occurred at the dropping of a poor member, on a certain Sunday of the last century. He had, unwittingly, dropped a quarter of a dollar into the box, and upon discovery of the unintentional and sapping draft upon his very limited finances, called early on Monday to state his grievance to the pastor, at the same time asking for his change, when 1*s.* 9*d.* was restored to him, leaving one penny and a half as his quota to the treasury of the church.

* Pennsylvania currency.

Economy, frugality, and measured ability, were bound by the silver cords of contentment, and were fully met by the representative of his church—the *pastor loci*, of whom there could be none more entitled to note than he, whose profile here witnesses this concession and tribute to his memory.

Rev. *John Meder*

CHAPTER XIV.

Brother John Meder—His Character—Anecdote—Costume and Classes Designated—a Glimpse of the Requirements in Bethlehem.

Brother John Meder possessed all the qualifications of a self-sacrificing missionary. Industry, perseverance, forbearance, and faithful continuance in well-doing, were cardinal virtues in this faithful servant of God.

He was a man small of stature, light built, and of doubtful constitution. Yet he was indefatigable in the performance of his duties, which were not only clerical, but domestic and secular.

He preached regularly twice on Sundays, calling the youth of his congregation, after afternoon service, to his shrine for catechization and special religious instruction; the pleasurable reference to which rejuvenates the reality as I cast my mind's eye to my post before him, and, even now, see the old gentleman leaning on his table, inspiring confidence in the timid youth, and conciliating fear, to counteract the difference between the catechist and the catechumen.

Besides these Sunday services, he held a meeting two evenings in the week, to wit, Wednesday and Friday, and in addition, performed all the parochial duties incumbent upon him, to the sick, the well, the dead, or the dying.

To his domestic affairs he was no less assiduous; a strict regard to economy drew upon his physical powers, but the drafts were paid promptly, and in full, from the spare moments of his parochial cares.

His garden was a beauty-spot in his realm, and its fragrance, its tasteful arrangements, and fruitful bearing, were florid evidences of his untiring industry; and yet with all this active and laborious devotion to his duties, no ill sprang up to mar or counteract his vigor.

The meek and unassuming bearing of this old gentleman was almost proverbial, and the relief to a subdued mind was very seldom sought in laughter; indeed, it was said that he never did laugh, but frequently quoted the preacher, "I said of laughter, It is mad, and of mirth, What doeth it?" Yet let me assure the reader that he was no drone, nor was he chilling in his mien by a disciplined sanctimonious rigidity.

As before stated, the parsonage was a large building, and so arranged that brethren visiting the city might there be provided for, and hence its proper name was the "Brethren's House." Tradition, and it is very direct, gives a pithy anecdote of the simplicity of an old-time brother. Such a one being then and there hospitably entertained, shortly after his first arrival in the city, left the house after tea, for the purpose of taking an evening walk. The pastor, of course, awaited an early return, for the city was not then very extensive. Time passed on, wasting patronage and patience. Nine o'clock was the usual hour for retirement, yet ten came, but not the absent brother. Fear and trembling beset the patient pastor, when eleven o'clock announced its proximity to midnight, yet no Brother S——.

The old gentleman nearly worn to a lethargy was suddenly aroused by the significant tap of the ponderous iron knocker. It was the stray brother.

"Dear brother," said the kindly host, "in all the world, where have you been, till this time of night?"

"Why," said the delinquent, "I walked up one street and down another, and saw in one of them, a place all lit up, and I went in to see what it meant. It was very pretty; pictures changed from one thing to another,—all sorts of dress,—music, and all sorts of queer doings. I staid till they were done, and was amused without thinking of time."

This woke the old gentleman to a pungent, but pastoral reproof.

"My brother," said he, "you have been in the playhouse! an indulgence entirely forbidden to professing Christians;" and a befitting lecture ensued.

This is neither cant, nor caprice, but a specimen of old-time simplicity and *naïveté.*

The inimitable Goldsmith has depicted the portrait of *our* pastor in the character of *his*, of the Deserted Village; and I, therefore, adopt it, as a beautifully graphic concentration of his virtues:

> "Unskilful he to fawn, or seek for power,
> By doctrines fashioned to the varying hour;
> For, other aims his heart had learned to prize,
> More bent to *raise* the wretched, than to rise."

It was the privilege of your author to receive the rite of Holy Baptism at the hands of this venerable servant of God (anno 1792), and to experience in after-life the fervency of his supplications, as he mingled them with his benediction, in his offerings at the baptismal font.

I cannot pass this point of my history, without a respectful notice of the good wife, the helpmate of this house. Meek, mild, modest, and unassuming, this lady matronized her department to the credit of her church, and the plenary comforts of her guests. Her duties were not confined to domestic economy, but were expanded to services of the parish, besides the incumbency of serving at the Holy Communion; she, taking the sister's side, whilst her husband, the minister, served the brethren. Unadorned by fancy or fashion, her apparel was chaste and simplified. A calico short-gown, calamanco petticoat, a white linen apron, and a "long-eared cap," were the accepted weekday offering of her presence; but *hers*, the usual full Moravian Sunday attire, requires an artist to depict; which I present, not as a *likeness* of Sister Meder, except in costume; the portrait itself having been made some years ago, by the Rev. Wm. Henry Van Vleck, the pastor of this church, from 1814 to 1820, as a likeness of his mother, and as for such I offer my attest, having been well acquainted with her fifty years ago, and long after.

This costume was not confined to that day, though more general amongst the sisters than it has been since, *i. e.*, in the country congregations. It was obligatory till 1819, when the governing power at Herrnhuth, giving heed to an appeal for one less peculiar, option was permitted to propitiate compulsion, and the rule, as such, was abrogated.

Notwithstanding the privilege to abandon, many of the elder sisters adhered to their pristine taste, and the cap, and the smooth, three-cornered kerchief may yet be seen in the congregation places,* contrasting the beauty of simplicity with the wayward fancy of the *march of improvement.*

In those days, besides the *separation* of the sexes, they were divided into choirs or classes, and designated by the color of the cap-tie. The widows wore a white ribbon to their caps; the married women, a blue; the single sisters, a pink; and the great girls, of twelve to sixteen years of age, red.

The brethren had, also, their denomination as widowers, married and single brethren, great boys (Knaben), who, though not in our day, designated by colors of any peculiar hue, had then their respective department in the congregational arrangements; and, like the sisters, had their respective and special festivals.

There was, however, a time, when the wilderness on the Lehigh was receding, and yielding its forest to the axe, the wedge, and the hammer; and the earth's bowels were wrought for the health and power of its wealth; when Bethlehem was started to the surface, from its hidden sources—the earliest day of Moravianism in America—then, at and about that time, the colored ribbon *did* tell what party might be their owner, so that when certain habiliments were doomed to ablution, they might pass the legitimate ordeal.

Two of the early patrons of this settlement (Brethren), were yet living, in 1833 and 1834, and often entertained me with legends of their day, and doings; the one as *washerwoman*, the other as laborer in the quarries.

* Country congregations, Bethlehem, Nazareth, Litiz, &c.

The widows, single sisters, and single brethren, having their own separate houses, called "Choir Houses," conducted their domestic economy within their immediate sphere; and direct intercourse between the sexes being interdicted, intermediate association was rendered impracticable by an absolute non-intercourse of their habiliments; and hence, the important office of washerwoman was conferred upon my ancient friend, a native of Bethlehem, of 1758. The other, also an associate with its very infancy, although ten years younger than the first named.

In all this we have a sample of the self-sacrificing principle and unsophisticated simplicity of the young brethren to identify themselves, and grow up with the then infant Bethlehem.

Dollars and cents were not a consideration; they worked for and through each other; and the common treasury furnished the ordinary; for, like the Apostles, "they had all things in common."

CHAPTER XV.

Chapel Servants—Jacob Frank—Jacob Ritter, Sr.—Zachariah Poulson, the Elder—Sketches of Character—Duties—Performances, Inviters, &c.

THE interregnum just passed, having its link somewhere in the sequel, I again take up the thread of my history, and pass on to the more immediate associations of offices and officers of the time before us.

The chapel servants were volunteer sextons, and served in turn, according to agreement amongst themselves.

Two, however, were usually in service every Sunday; the one sat on the wall bench, behind the men's door, for the purpose of waiting on strangers, and also to watch the boys who might attempt to go into the gallery. The other, on the wall bench, at the door opening into the church from the parsonage, for the purpose, as before stated, of waiting on the minister, as well as to watch the occasionally restive and tittering youth, as they ranged with his eye, in front of the pulpit. Of these brethren, no menial services were required.

The housemaid of the parsonage, included the service of making the fire in the stove, bringing up wood, sweeping and sanding the floor, aye, and unfastening the church doors, and opening the gate on Race Street; all in her wages of five shillings,—67 cents a week.

The scrubbing of the floor, however, and washing of

windows, was by order of, and paid for by the committee.

But it was ever and anon, "a nicely sanded floor," and was a credit to the watchful eye and ready hand that kept it so; and "Kate," though a housemaid, being faithful to her trust, fairly deserves a line in the annals of her church. "Honor to whom honor is due."

This female functionary filled the station, as well that of *femme de chambre* as *chef de la cuisine*, besides venting her ambition on the church and its furniture, for upwards of twenty years; most of the time, at the aforesaid 5*s*. per week—the usual wages of the day—but subsequently raised to 7*s*. 6*d*., or $1 per week, and no choice as to what she would, or what she would not do. The march of improvement had not yet reversed domestic economy, and refined the maid to educate the mistress.

Of the chapel servants, after Brother John Mark, who served for two years, a venerable and kindly brother, Jacob Frank, being the first regularly appointed, in December, 1787, is justly entitled to respectful notice and perpetuity.

Having served in this capacity, and other useful offices in the church, for upwards of thirty years, he covers my time, and furnishes data from the liveliest recollections.

There is not a boy or girl, who sat upon the low bench in front of the table, that, were he or she yet here, would not bear happy testimony to the friendly mien of this old gentleman; and when his significant "Boys!" came out, it came kindly. Terror was not in his breath, nor fear from its issue. None feared him; all loved him, and one gentle "Boys!" was enough.

He was wont to parade up and down before us, calmly

watching our movements, and especially preparatory to love-feast; placing us according to age, and sometimes size, but never according to fractions,—dollars and cents. He was impartial in his attentions; but naturally regarded those most, who behaved best.

His olive breeches, of velvet or corduroy, brindled stockings, and shoes to fit the foot; his dark brown coat, and copious vest, pass, even now, before me with their venerable charge of thoughtful, truthful, and suavitous bearing, and revive a happy, and an almost tangible reminiscence.

Mr. Frank was a tanner by trade, and lived at the southwest corner of Fourth and Noble Streets, a hollow then, being the terminus of the declivity from Callowhill Street; a lonely, and very disagreeable walk; which I sometimes had to do after night; and as often exercised my musical powers, by whistling up my courage at every step.

He departed this life, November 26, 1819, aged 76 years, 1 month, and 15 days.

The next in immediate connection with this service, was my own venerable and dearly beloved sire; whose plain apparel, very like that just described, except that he wore silver buckles, was adorned with a godly inheritance, freely beaming from a countenance evidently at peace with God and man. It does not, however, behoove me here to set him forth; but I may, and I do, most sincerely, thank God for his existence, and its salutary influence upon my moral and religious bearing, thus far through life. His walks and conduct bore testimony to the meditations of his heart; consistency with his profession being his conscientious study.

Having been an early member of the Society, almost in its embryo, admitted as such after a considerable contest with his father, who was a Lutheran, and also a man of piety, in July, 1774, I take the liberty of presenting the annexed very correct copy from a portrait by the late J. F. Krimmel, in 1818.

He departed this life, November 3d, 1834, aged 80 years, less 15 days.

We have, however, another contemporary in this department, in the person and services of Zachariah Poulson.

This old gentleman was appointed in 1801, and served till 1804,—the time of his death. A countenance on which nature had shed its bounty, was ever enhanced and lit up by the evidences of a happy train of mental associations.

His commands were "few and far between," but not the less known. The serenity of his countenance conveyed his desires in the calm of his kindly smile.

Mr. Poulson was the father of the late Zachariah Poulson, editor and proprietor of Poulson's American Daily Advertiser.

He was a native of Copenhagen, in Denmark, born 16th of June, 1737, but immigrated to this country in 1749, with his father, whose name was Nicholas Poulson, also a printer.

Our Mr. Poulson was a widower and lived with his son, the editor.*

* I am indebted to his grandson, Mr. C. A. Poulson, for the following historical sketch of his venerable sire.

Zachariah Poulson, my paternal grandfather, was born in Copenhagen, the metropolis of Denmark, on the 16th day of June, A.D. 1737. His

His apparel was light drab, plain cut coat, and breeches in old-time fashion. Suspenders were not known; but he, and his colleagues in the church service, were all plain Quaker-dressed brethren.

These were a trio of Christian gentlemen, exemplars

father, Nicholas Poulson, or Paulsens (as I find it written by him in documents in my possession), after the decease of his wife, emigrated, on account of his religion, to this country, with his only child (Zachariah), and arrived in the city of Philadelphia, Pa., in the year 1749. He died at Germantown a few years thereafter.

My grandfather was a printer. He was taught the art by the celebrated Christopher Sower, a German printer, (spelt, in the German language, *Sauer*. It seems to have been the fashion in those days, to anglicise foreign names), then a resident of Germantown, Pa. Sower, like his great predecessor, Faust, manufactured his own materials—types, printing ink, paper, &c. He printed the *first edition* of the Holy Bible published in the United States; it is in the German language. He issued from his press three editions of that work, viz., in 1743, 1762, and 1776; the greater portion of the latter, in his possession, was confiscated during the Revolutionary War, and used as cartridge paper.

My grandfather married Anna Barbara Stallenberger, daughter of Andrew, of that name, late of Lindenbach, near Wertheim Leibenstein, Germany. He (the latter) likewise emigrated from his native land for the enjoyment of religious freedom, after having sold his property. He died three days before the arrival of the vessel, and was buried at New Castle, Delaware. "He was eminent for his piety, and other good qualities." His family arrived at Philadelphia, and settled at Germantown, in the year 1752.

My grandfather deceased in Philadelphia on the 4th of June, 1804. It is recorded of him, "that he has always been esteemed, by those who knew him, for his integrity, for the sincerity and ardor of his friendship, and for his amiable and inoffensive deportment." He departed this life with that resignation and humble confidence which is inspired by religion and the consciousness of a well-spent life. His remains were borne to the cemetery of the Moravian Church by his brethren of the typographical art, and interred in the presence of a considerable number of his relations.

of their profession, unblemished in character, and unsoiled of evil report, and even yet form an entablature in the vista of time, a light to its perspective, and a sweet-smelling savor to the avenue of fondling memory.

There were two other important appendages to church-government, or rather outside regulations, to wit: a Grave-digger, and an Inviter. History claims their manes, and though minor in capacity, they belong to the compass of our times.

A certain Jacob Ettwein performed the silent duty of preparing the pit. He was appointed, March, 1786, but it appears from the records, that his inattention to his duties, becoming *employer*, instead of *employed*, begat him censure and threats of discharge.

The most important official in this department was the Inviter. This office required more intelligence than that of his associate's finale, the preface to which must be set forth not only intelligibly but geographically.

Typography was not yet the "*multum in parvo*," nor penmanship "*au fait*," at a moment's warning. Invitations were, therefore, neither printed nor written, nor yet a fleet and elastic "Bogle," to trip over the pave and bounce from step to step, to distribute the respectful civilities of mourning friends.

The respective churches had their respective Inviters, who with note in one hand and cane in the other, with measured step, passed from house to house, gave the significant tap of the knocker, awaited the call, and then in sober, qualified tone, thus relieved himself:

"This family is particularly invited to attend the funeral of S. S., from his late dwelling, No. —, North or South —— Street, to-morrow afternoon, at 3 o'clock."

This message was generally a curt expression, but sometimes a loquacious vein would spin the pedigree of the subject, to the enlightenment or edification of the very willing, and perhaps inquisitive listener.

The Moravian Church, being as yet circumscribed in numbers, had none in their immediate circle to serve in this capacity, and they, therefore, employed this functionary of the German Lutheran Church, and Henry Cress became this incumbent in 1795. How long he served, our history saith not; but that George Gossner, a dapper little, friendly, gentlemanly man, also of the Lutheran Church, was a successor in this office, came within my own knowledge, is as certain as the record of the former.

In whatever light this occupation may be viewed nowadays, it was not without tone then; and good manners and respectable character were indispensable in the applicant. To this record bears evidence, in its tale of rejection of some less available.

CHAPTER XVI.

The Burial-Ground—Order of Services, &c.

THIS depository was purchased and thus appropriated, as before stated, in 1757. The lot appears to have been unprotected, except by post and rail fence, till 1786, when order was taken by the Committee of the Church "to purchase four thousand feet of New England pine boards, to make a board fence, around our burying-ground," of which report was rendered, and account of particulars stated, amounting to *50l.* 11*s.* 3*d.*, which sum, as the brethren always counted the cost of the undertakings in advance, was immediately gathered and paid.

As death levels all of life, ornamental or distinctive memorabilia were not allowed to disturb the simple uniformity of the tokens of remembrance; the marble slab was even limited in its length and breadth, to twelve by eighteen inches, and these all flat, on the mound that heaves to the eye, the silent but imposing "Memento Mori."

So fastidious were the guardians of this order, even so late as 1820, that a considerable sacrifice was made to principle, in the refusal of a vault to a wealthy contributor, for an after consideration of $7500.

This principle, however, has since fallen a prey to

caprice, and various sizes of affection's tablet, dispute the palm of the earlier, well-ordered, and more simple tokens of affection.

Although the church was located so far from the burying-ground, it appears to have been customary to carry the corpse of the deceased to the church, for the benefit of the funeral rites, and a succinct biography was first read. In 1789, however, the practice was discontinued; and the services requested to be performed at the grave.*

The streets in this section of the Northern Liberties, being as yet not graded, left the plot considerably above the level, and hence the difference at this day, between the one and the other. The grade, however, appears to have been made in 1805; allusion being then made to it, and resolutions passed, to "remove the fence and erect a brick wall," which was done; and stood without spring or warp until 1856; when taste, judgment, fancy, and liberality conspired against it, and the march of improvement *did actually* offer an amendment to the resolve of our fathers; the better to harmonize with the spirit of the age, as the present new church edifice, and its illustrated appurtenances, more elaborately set forth.

The erect permanence and durability of this wall, for half a century, was a wonder to very many inquirers, its visible thickness being only nine inches on Franklin Street, and scant thirteen inches on Vine Street; but the recent removal of the wall disclosed the secret, in a stubborn inner wall of stone, of about two feet in height, and

* In the town or congregation places, this custom yet prevails, in which the deceased having kept an account of himself, his biography is read; or a general history from other sources is given, but the funeral service is read at the grave.

one foot thick, intended no doubt as an additional support to the ground, so far above the street level; serving, however, the double purpose of protecting the outer wall; and this base, thanks to the wisdom of our fathers, continues its service behind the new wall, perpetuating their memory and confirming our acknowledgments.

This ground was purchased, by the congregation of 1757, and conveyed to it, for the special use of its actual church members, and such persons as stand in religious society, or otherwise, in connection with them.

To such, therefore, there was no charge made for breaking the ground, the grave-digger and the inviter being the only beneficiaries of this department, the former receiving three dollars for each grave, and the latter, one dollar for his prior services, and his safe conduct of the respectful and sympathizing train, for the inviter always preceded the cortege.

Despite the rule, there were many urging relationship, however remote, and claiming rights by a sort of collateral inheritance, which being unprofitable, as it was troublesome, a rigid observance of the rule became necessary,—a very important protective system over such limited means.

CHAPTER XVII.

The Discipline.

Associations, moral, religious, or political, must of necessity be subject to a proper discipline; and, whether gentle or severe, a due observance is incumbent upon its members.

A religious society, however, being the especial safeguard of doctrine, according to godliness and consequent sound principles, accountability is exacted of it, and jealousy of a consistent bearing and characteristic example of its body, demands a watchful care over its spiritual possessions.

Unfledged in worldly waywardness, but of demeanor imbued with Christian simplicity, these early brethren strove earnestly to keep themselves in "the unity of the Spirit, and the bond of peace;" and, to this end, their requirements were, although rigid, the essence of uprightness of thought and intention; yet, however administered, in all meekness and forbearance.

The absence of record, for the first forty years of their social existence, debars me aught of written or printed dates touching this order of things; but the rays of their light had beggared time, and sped their genial influence into the hearts and minds of their successors, whilst the halo of their spiritual might lit up a path to their future footsteps.

Whilst theatres were repudiated as a "school of morals," dancing was denounced as a consideration for healthful exercise; balls were not allowed as a relish to the trials of life, nor caprices of any sort permitted to excite the palate to a depraved appetite.

Politics or political associations were discountenanced and held as amongst the "evil communications that corrupt good manners."

The society consisted nearly, if not quite all, of communicant members, who were, therefore, a guard and a check to each other; but the supervision was in the Bishop and his ministers, who spared not the rod to spoil the "babe in Christ;" hence, when a brother accidentally fell into a gap in his profession, and the mysterious lights allured him whither he else would not, the goodly shepherd sheared him at once of the soft and woolly covering of his apologies, and bid him to sin no more in that way. Up to a certain time, these observances needed no enactment; the law was in their hearts, and they were "a law unto themselves."

The watchful care of the venerable Bishop Ettwein, however, was called to an exordium, in 1795, by a sideling of some of his flock in Lancaster, into the political arena, and the Conference at Bethlehem, through him, to the committee of the church in Philadelphia, deplore the dereliction of "some of the brethren in Lancaster, who had joined a political body called Democrats, and even accepted of office therein; such conduct being inconsistent with not only good order, but with the rules laid down for us by our Saviour."

They, the Conference, "therefore exhort the brethren not to meddle in any political affairs and controversies, but rather strive to seek the peace of the places wherein we dwell."

Well, indeed, would it be, had *all* the clergy kept this faith; well for their own peace, and well for their flocks.

Political excitement is, at best, disaffecting in church and state; but, when the herald of the Cross becomes a champion for fancied political rights, takes his stand on the curb, or is jostled to the ballot-box, amidst the excited opposition of jeers and gibes, chafed by an opposing member of his own church, his clerical influence must be scathed of the softness of its sanctity, whilst his early vows are lost, for the time, in the vapor of political strife.

It is true, many worthy, highly respected, and lovely ministers of the Gospel have considered their elective franchise a national blessing, and an important duty, but without much research, even they could not be advised of the arcana of politics, but their pulpits remained also unadvised, whilst to their charge below or abroad, their sentiments were a dead letter.

In all this, I do not deny rights and privileges to the clergy; but the *expediency* of the exercise of these immunities is questionable when the "peace of our Jerusalem" is at stake, and "the peace of the places wherein we dwell is in danger of suffocation in the angry fumes of political exhalations." St. Paul says, "All things are lawful for me, but all things are not expedient."

Parties were not admissible as a medium to discount time, or an amusing expedient to nurse the day in the bosom of the night.

They were not allowed as propitiatory offerings to the

ordinary duties of the day, nor countenanced as a balancing power of the day-worn mind.

Nor yet was the social circle impugned! Hospitality was not at bay, nor friendly associations chilled by the frowns of a sanctimonious brow.

Religion did not make their pleasures less; but their desires were regulated by it, whilst their conceptions were chastened by its influence.

Their evening gatherings were pleasurable arrangements, and the social tea-cup passed from hand to hand, without the aid of a sable attendant.

Their festivity consisted more in sentimental passes than luxurious offerings; whilst the needle, or even the spindle, gave a zest to the "flight of time."

Four P.M. was late to begin, and nine full time to end.

In those days, day was day; evening was evening; and night was night.

It must, however, be conceded that, "the spirit of the age" had not given birth to nocturnal embellishments as of the present day, but what may have been rife of fanciful exhibitions, were disallowed as obnoxious to the observance due to the moral, as well as the religious, bearing of the society.

Nor can it be denied, that even within these limits there were some untoward subjects. Nay, Time's telltale, History, says there were; but they did not pass the ordeal of the pastorate.

Dereliction from the path of rectitude was dealt with firmly, but in the "spirit of meekness;" but contumacy resulted in expulsion from the society.

To this end a special, but private meeting of the Congregation (communicants) was held in the hall, where good reasons were given, and the difficult member was "read out of meeting."

To these proceedings my duties as bellows-boy, in the beginning of the present century, necessarily made me a witness.

The paucity of members was no bar to the execution of their laws; nor were they so subject to the "unhappy desire of becoming great" as to increase their numbers by proselytism or improper indulgence.

Fruit of their labor was certainly desirable, and they as certainly sought it; but it must needs be good fruit, gleanings from the chaff of the world.

It was, therefore, not so easy to be admitted into their society, and yet more trying to be admitted into close Communion. Applicants were required to wait six months before they could be received, and then only after a walk and demeanor consistent with their religious intentions, besides the *pastoral* of the minister in various private interviews during this probation. Candidates for the Holy Communion were more scrutinously examined, and were required to *understand themselves*, before they could be fully introduced to that circle; but, as the Conference at Bethlehem was the *senatus consultum* and a guard over all their outer churches, their application had first to pass that ordeal, under the direction of the lot, in which the Conference "made known to God, their wants, by prayer and supplication" (of which, more in its order). There were, therefore, *very few* delinquents in this infant society, not over three being noted in the first sixty years of its being, and these were not close members. The expulsions, alluded to heretofore, belong to the present century.

The Bishop made frequent visits to the church, for whom the Standing Committee was always immediately convened, and a kindly investigation into the spiritual state of the congregation, as well as a sympathy with its temporal affairs, was entered into, and in conformity with our Saviour's injunction to his disciples, to "love one another," the Bishop's first inquiry was, "Brethren, do you love one another in sincerity?" thus simplifying instead of sublimating his prelacy.

Under such and corresponding influences of the rulers of the church, the Discipline, however peculiar, was accepted and observed, more as a conjugal requirement, than an Egyptian task.

The corresponding influences flowed from the rites and ceremonies of the Church, and the careful example of its rulers, who fully practised what they preached, or, as David has it in his 106th Psalm, thus rendered:

"Happy are they, and only they,
Who from thy judgments never stray,
Who know what's right, nor only so,
But always practise what they know."

CHAPTER XVIII.

The Pedelavium, or Washing of Feet.

THE Moravians, individually and collectively, being evangelical, beyond compromise, took very literally the example of the Saviour as their guide, and claimed its furtherance by his early disciples and Apostles, as their countenance and support.

The Washing of Feet was, therefore, adopted and practised literally, as enjoined by the Divine Master, 13th John, 4, 5: "He riseth from supper, and laid aside his garments, and took a towel and girded himself; after that, he poureth water into a basin, and began to wash his disciples' feet, and to wipe them with the towel wherewith he was girded."

This example of humility was practised immediately before the administration of the Lord's Supper, and was fully supported, as a proper observance, by the Evangelist's record: "Ye call me Master and Lord, and ye say well, for so I am. If I, then, your Lord and Master, have washed your feet, ye ought also to wash one another's feet. For I have given you an example, that ye should do as I have done to you."—Verses 13, 14, 15, of the above chapter. All which having been said and done by our Saviour, at the time of his Supper, the Moravian

Church adopted the same, as the proper time for particular attention to the example.

This was a solemn rite, and solemly performed, and was a corresponding influence calculated to chasten the moral turpitude of the natural man, else, uprising to the prejudice and waste of the beauty of holiness.

The custom, however, was limited to the older brethren and sisters, in whom Christian experience was ripe, and to whom the junior members looked, under the Gospel, for the savor of life unto life.

It was not regarded as a positive command, and therefore, not observed as a sacrament, nor as an institution, but as a recommendation of our Saviour to humility, and moral and religious equality. Ye ought also to wash one another's feet; "the servant is not greater than his Lord, nor he that is sent, greater than he that sent him."

This elder class, having diminished by death to some five or six members, and the privacy necessary to the accomplishment of this purpose annulled by the destruction of the hall of the first church, in 1819–20, the observance became impracticable, and was discontinued, more of necessity than of choice; but there is now not one living member of that humble few.

CHAPTER XIX.

The Holy Communion—Kiss of Peace—Doctrine of the Sacrament.

THIS sacred ordinance is a fundamental principle in the Moravian Church, as it doubtless is in all other Christian Churches; but its observance in the form and administration is thought to be more impressive and more interesting.

In the first place, it is entirely private, and no disturbance whatever could find its way into the assemblage.

Strangers were not admitted, except on application to the minister, and then only such as were communicants elsewhere, or persons of known Christian bearing.

Secondly. The administration of the elements is accompanied by the Hymnology of the Church, especially adapted to the solemnity of this service, so that whilst the minister is in the act of distribution, passing from bench to bench, silently handing the bread and the wine to each individual, the whole congregation are commemorating the death of Jesus, in sacred harmony; following the subdued tones of the organ, with "melody in their hearts."

After the distribution of the bread, and the minister has pronounced the Saviour's command, "Take, eat," &c., a silent prayer (the congregation kneeling) ensues; whilst the mellowing influence of the organ mingles its suasive powers to wing their contrite aspirations to the throne of grace,—a most beautiful and imposing observance in the administration.

After the introductory address and prayer, there is nothing said beyond the Scripture warrant and command for the observance. The hymning of praise, prayer, and supplication constitute the actual service.

Preparatory to this service, it was the practical duty of the minister, either to visit his communicant members, for the purpose of a particular knowledge of their spiritual state, or to have a special meeting in the church, for "instruction in righteousness," by advice, solicitude, or consolation; and this was a happy medium to the altar, of special communication with the Redeemer's sacrifice, and was not without effect, to enlighten the mind and warm the heart to the things that belonged to their peace. This custom was a species of confession, though not by any means in the full sense of the Roman Catholic Church.

It was as well a custom of the Lutheran Church, and there called "beught," which means confession, but by the Moravians "sprechen," or speaking, and was a medium of discharging the mind of unhallowed influences, and the opportunity to "confess your faults, one to another," and to "pray one for another." It gave the communicant an opportunity of improvement, by a special spiritual intercourse with his pastor, for there was a fair exchange of sentiment, and the confessor was not the silent recipient of the secrets of his subject, but the companion in arms, assisting his weak brother in "the good fight of faith," that his "man of God might be perfect," thoroughly furnished unto all good works.

The increase of members, in all probability, encumbered the pastor above his ability, and the custom was compromised of necessity, and concentrated into a "preparatory meeting," held on the Sunday afternoon next before the celebration, when singing, prayer, and address, all touching the religious bearing of communicants especially, were solemnly enacted; and the warning, the admonition, and the encouraging exordium passed from pious lips to hearts and minds open to conviction, and ready to be "established in the faith." (Acts, 16:5.)

THE KISS OF PEACE.

The late venerable Bishop Spangenberg, an early father of our Church, writes, on this subject, thus:

"Paul writes to the Romans, 16:16, 'Salute one another with a holy kiss,' and refers further to 1 Corinth. 16:20, 2 Corinth. 13:12; 1 Thess. 26, and Peter 1:14, 'Greet ye one another with the kiss of charity;'" and proceeds, "This act must certainly have been of importance to the disciples of Jesus, as it is repeated by them more than once.

"Not amongst the Jews only, but amongst other nations also, it was customary for one man to testify the love and regard he had for another by a kiss.

"Our Saviour, therefore, reminds the Pharisee, who had invited him, that he had not received him with a kiss.

"Of consequence, our Lord Jesus Christ would have received a kiss from a Pharisee.

"But it is probable, in the Apostolical Churches, besides the kiss used in common life, with which one man received or dismissed the other, this kiss was made use of in their meetings."—See Exposition of Christian Doctrine of the Unitas Fratrum, by A. G. Spangenberg, p. 251.

This ancient custom of the Christian Church was continued in the Moravian Church, and constituted an affectionate and interesting feature in the celebration of the Lord's Supper in America until very recently, where it has been discontinued in most of the congregations; a good reason for which, it would be difficult to find!

It was a mutual salutation of the congregation, the very best evidence of good fellowship; and an earnest of the Apostle's injunction, to be "Kindly affectioned to one another."

The brethren and sisters being separated in their sittings, it was free from any danger whatever of abuse; and this separation was not confined to this portion of the Christian Church, seeing that the deacon of ancient times, after certain preliminary ceremonies, "cried out aloud, Mutually embrace and kiss each other."—See Eucharist, in Buck's Theological Dictionary.

It is certainly lamentable, that the spirit of the age should be encouraged to bring into subjection the patience, the purity, and the Christian simplicity of the saints of the early age.

They were not ashamed of this evidence of love to each other, nor did they fear or regard derision from a benighted observer.

Like David, they washed their hands in innocency, and embraced each other in purity.

"Say, my peace I leave with you;
Amen, Amen, be it so,"

was the melody of their hearts, after rising from prayer, and as they offered the salutation, at the conclusion, was

" Once more we pledge both heart and hand,
As in God's presence here we stand,"—

the pledge of friendship and Christian fellowship, in the kindly "kiss of peace."

Personal objections have been urged as available reason for the disuse of the custom; but is this not a sad confession of refinement against Christian simplicity? There never was any evil in it, but a decided medium of good; and yet the *Unitas Fratrii*, if not the only church, certainly one of the few that adopted and continued it as good for more than a century, now abandon it, in accordance with the spirit of the age, as inconvenient, and to the world unseemly.

To our sister churches, who never saw it in our light, we have nothing to object; but in those who saw it for good, adopted it as a silken cord to Christian unity, drank from the golden bowl of its fructifying laver, and refreshed themselves in the odor of its purity, wonder must ever exist, and regret swell the bosom of the most casual observer, at the discontinuance of so interesting a distinctive feature of a Christian church.

THE DOCTRINES OF THE SACRAMENT.

The materials used in the celebration of the Lord's Supper are, as instituted by our Saviour, "bread and wine;"—wafer, or unleavened bread, made expressly for the occasion, but not common bread.

The various differences amongst Christians, as to the specific substance of the Eucharist, appears not to be mooted, but rather compromised in the Moravian Church; for, whilst transubstantiation appears too positive and dogmatical, consubstantiation seemed too indefinite, and quite as hard to be understood.

The Church, therefore, had no dogma on this doctrine; but, taking the words of our Saviour, the participant receives it according to his faith, to which a more than ordinary blessing attaches, in proportion to the spiritual subduing of the natural man.

To say that it *is* the real presence, other than in a spiritual sense, is, perhaps, assuming too much; whilst to say that it is *not*, necessarily enlists, and always arrays human wisdom against Almighty power, and doubtful disputations ensue.

The Church, taking the Scriptures exclusively as its guide, without reference to compilations from various, and perhaps biassed construction, has ever conformed as near to their literal import as possible; and hence, to avoid error in its fundamental principles, did not adopt anything as a dogma that was calculated to cause controversy. Hence, no question was elicited on the subject of the character or nature of the elements in the Communion, after the consecration at the altar.

Faithfulness in the ministerial act, and faith in the recipients, leave it an open question, that "every man may be fully persuaded in his own mind."

The ordinance is certainly not of common origin, and cannot be viewed as an ordinary or periodical celebration. It was instituted by Christ himself, and that, too, in his human nature; but it was under the influence of a perfect man, whose blessing, hallowed in an especial manner by the Father, imparted more of a Divine essence than ordinary human nature could give.

There was, therefore, no possibility of the shadow of a thought incompatible with the purity of the aspirations; and hence, we have every reason to confide in a corresponding return from the Source of life and light.

Divinity, therefore, shed its power over that repast, and this influence can have lost nothing in the lapse of time; so that, as before observed, a more than ordinary degree of spiritual enjoyment precedes the commemora tion of Christ's sufferings and death, by a proper preparation, and follows it by a faithful observance; and whether it be Transubstantiation or Consubstantiation, it is the communion of the body and blood of Christ, under the scriptural direction; or, as the Princess Elizabeth of England answered, when pressed for a confession of her faith:

> "Christ was the word that spake it.
> He took the bread and brake it,
> And what that word did make it,
> That I believe, and take it."

Nor is this answer as evasive, as at first sight might appear.

> "And what that word did make it,"

is fraught with depth of thought and meaning. It was a Divine word, and though passing human lips, it bedewed the atmosphere of the scene with an unction, especially sanctifying

> "The word that spake it."

In reference to the influence of the commemoration,

upon the spiritual sensibilities of the participant, the venerable John Aitken, a pious and exemplary member of Christ Church, who walked ten miles every first Sunday in the month, for this renewal of his inner man, used to say, that it built him up in his spiritual might, two weeks before, and two weeks after the celebration; "so that," said he, "I am built up all the time."

The subject is, at best, one of interminable difficulty, wherever and whenever human wisdom attempts a controversy; the *Unitas Fratrii*, therefore, avoiding the shoals of disputations, making no dogma, receive the elements of the Holy Communion in simplicity and faith, asking no questions.

In the administration of this sacrament, the minister wears a surplice, as, also, at the rite of Baptism and Confirmation; in the latter, however, not obligatory.

CHAPTER XX.

The Liturgy—Liturgies and Litanies of the Church.

This is a regular formula of a religious service, and comprises a compilation of hymns and sentences, for various special occasions; to wit, a special liturgy:

To the Father,
To the Son,
To the Holy Ghost,
To the Trinity,
To the passion of our Lord, &c.

In each, the sentiment of the hymns is specially adapted to the subject or object in view.

It is the melody of the heart, in psalms, and hymns, and spiritual songs.

The melody, however, is various; changing from fifteen to twenty tunes, in three-quarters of an hour.

Each liturgy constituted an evening service; and was sung in alternate strains by the minister or liturgus, the choir, Ch; the sisters, S; and the congregation, C; of which the following is a specimen:

L. "Christ, our Saviour, look on thee,
Ransomed congregation.
Ch. Thou art his, because that he,
Purchased thy salvation."

C. "We are his, through mercy. To him, our Saviour,
We'll humbly cleave, till we shall see him ever.
Hallelujah!"

L. and Ch. "To him be glory at all times; in the church which waiteth for him, and in that which is about him.
All. From everlasting to everlasting. Amen."

L. and Ch. "Now let all say, Amen. The Lord be praised
In heaven and earth, his name forever blessed
By all that breathe."

A. "Oh, did each pulse thanksgiving beat,
S. And every breath his praise repeat.
A. Amen. Hallelujah!
Ch. Hallelujah!
A. Amen. Hallelujah!"

L. and Ch. "Holy, holy, holy, In earth and heaven,
To God, and to the Lamb, be praises given,
In harmony."

This mode of worship is not only interesting, but delightful; and whilst I am writing, I am, in heart and voice, remodelling my early sensations; and, most happily, floating on the choral sea of the harmonious swell of a place or a country congregation.

Yes, the Religious and Moral Athenæum of Nazareth, may even yet whisper an echo, from its venerable walls, of praise, of prayer, and of supplication to the hoary head of an early pilgrim, who once, in the freshness of his vocal powers, impressed them with the fervor of his youthful spiritual zeal.

To strangers, however, this mode of worship was rather enigmatical, and when practised here, by some was hard to be understood. Such an one once happened in during one of these services, but though very fond of music, could take no part in this. He, however, abode his time; but, when the service was over, he stepped to a member and said, "That is a curious service; they are no sooner in a tune, than they are again out, and into another." "My dear friend," continued he, "that thing must be learned!"

In the Preface of the copy before me, issued in London, in 1793, the writer says, "This new edition of Liturgic Hymns, for the United Brethren's Congregation, containing Litanies and solemn Anthems, with some pieces belonging to the Ritual, has been occasioned partly by the necessity of a new revision of those Liturgic Hymns, which have been in use since 1770, and partly by repeated applications to have them enlarged." So that 1770 would appear as the date of its origin.

How long they were in use in the city congregations, there are no means of ascertaining, but I am happy to know that in the place congregations, they yet form a welded and harmonious link in the chain of Moravianism.

The unbroken service requires practical skill in the organist, to pass from one melody to another, without change of key, seeing that a succession of modulations would mar the service by efforts uninterestingly tame, or distressingly severe, besides the unnecessary consumption of time. He must, therefore, be able to pass on, connecting the harmony by a befitting interlude, or, if by a curt appeal to science, he can slip into the required change, he may do so; but, to the credit of the Moravian organists in general, it must be said, that they are equal to any emergency of their service.

THE LITANIES.

The Liturgies, being for the most part ascriptive of praise to the attributes of the Deity, were rendered into rhythmic harmony, whilst the Litanies were supplicatory, and rendered in paragraphic sentences, principally quotations from the Scriptures, interspersed with a small portion of singing.

Of these, there are also several, viz.:

The Church Litany, originally forming an early separate Sunday Morning Service; but, in after time and now constitutes a *part* of the *regular* Sunday Morning Service.

The Easter Morning Litany, constituting and comprising the Creed of the Church, is prayed regularly, and I am happy to believe *faithfully*, on Easter Morning, at 5 o'clock, after the reading of the history of the Resurrection. This Litany is particularly rich in composition, thoroughly scriptural, and deeply imposing, and cannot fail to carry the mind with it, from the beginning to the end. It and the Church Litany were original drafts of Zinzendorff, but remodelled by the Synod of Herrnhuth, and adopted by the Church.

Litanies at Baptisms, of which there are several, to wit:

For Children.

For Adults, and

For Adults from the Heathen.

In the two last, the candidate makes confession of his Faith.

Litanies at Burials, of which there were, and are yet, two, differing in form and length, solemnly beautified, by the introduction of several verses, to be sung by the attendants at the grave, ascending as the incense of homage to "the Lord, who gave," and to the same "Lord, who hath taken away."

The foregoing forms a part of the Ritual of the Church, in addition, however, there are formulas for

Confirmation,
Ordination, and
Doxologies.

The one doxology, a verse of ascription of praise to the Trinity at the close of *any* service.

The other, a specific ascription to the meritorious offerings of the Redeemer, in which the congregation take an alternate part, thus:

Minister.—Unto the Lamb that was slain,
Cong.—And hath redeemed us out of all nations of the earth, &c. &c.

CHAPTER XXI.

The Lot.

The Moravians were from the beginning a people of strong faith. They were Bible Christians to the letter, and scrutinously practical in their profession.

Our Saviour had said to his disciples, Luke 17 : 6, "If ye had faith as a grain of mustard seed, ye might say unto this sycamore tree, Be thou plucked up by the root, and be thou cast into the sea, and it should obey you."

This figure of speech, although very strong, was illustrative of the power of Faith.

"Elias prayed that it might not rain, and it did not rain; and again he prayed that it might rain, and it did rain." (James 5 : 17, 18.)

And the 11th chapter of Hebrews is a compendium of the wonderful workings of Faith. In a word, "Faith being the substance of things hoped for, and the evidence of things not seen" (Hebrews 11 : 1), "the Brethren sought a more direct medium of its exercise in an appeal to the Lot."

It was a custom of ancient date, from Leviticus to the Acts of the Apostles, and was appealed to as well for secular settlements, as for ecclesiastical consultation.

In the early stage of the Moravian Church, it was the umpire of all important questions, moral or religious.

Missions were established and ministers appointed under its directions, whilst matrimonial arrangements were decided by the yea or nay of the Lot.

It was a matter requiring strong Faith; yet Faith was there, and its results were satisfactory.

But it pleases God sometimes to try our Faith even by a contrary working of the answer given: this was but "pruning the tree, that it might bring forth more fruit," and so acknowledged by the faithful in the trial.

In all cases, the manifestations of truth followed the disappointment with spiritual light. And if the thing desired was negatived, or being granted, was not successful, it was but to make way for a better, as well as a perfecting of patience; or, in the language of the poet,

> "Good when he gives, supremely good,
> Nor less when he denies.
> Even crosses from his sovereign hand,
> Are blessings in disguise."

It was, and it ever will be, an answer to prayer, wherever it be the prayer of faith.

It was the strong arm of the Church, and threw its mantle over the earth; it ploughed the fallow ground of the North, and nourished the darksome regions of the South.

Without "purse or scrip," the missionaries went forth, in obedience to its mandate, and very many of "the people who had sat in darkness, saw a great light."

The following table of missionary stations of this Church, lately published in "The Moravian," a very ably edited organ of the Church, gives an elaborate view of the fruits of the faith reposed in the Lot, by which, knowing it to be the command of, or sanctioned by, the Most High, its appellees went forth to the work with "full purpose of heart," and were "blessed in their deed," to which the following statistics are in point.

Table containing the Numerical Result of the Missionary Labors of the Moravian Church, about the middle of the year 1856.

Provinces and Stations.		Date of Establishment.	Communicants.	Baptized Adults.	Baptized Children.	Total in Church Fellowship.	Total in each Island or Colony.	Candidates for Baptism, New People, and Excluded.	Total under Instruction in the Stations.	Total in each Island or Colony.	Total under the several Governments.	National Numbers.
NORTH AMERICA.												
GREENLAND.	New Herrnhut,	1733	221	33	124	378		38	416			
	Lichtenfels,	1758	177	78	109	364	1,852		364	2,053	2,053	2,053 Greenlanders.
	Lichtenau,	1774	254	136	250	640		98	738			
	Fredericksthal,	1824	236	68	166	470		65	535			
LABRADOR.	Nain,	1771	98	78	96	272		15	287			
	Okak,	1776	122	59	107	288	1,084	15	301	1,221	1,221	1,221 Esquimaux.
	Hopedale,	1782	70	78	108	256		29	285			
	Hebron,	1830	80	77	111	268		78	346			
DELAWARES.	New Fairfield,	1792	38	50	80	168		37	205			
	Westfield,	1838	40	21	60	121	416	12	133	486		
CHEROKEES.	N. Spring Place,	1801	26	11	18	55		11	66		486	
	Canaan and Mt. Zion,	1843	29		43	72		10	82			539 Indians.
CENT. AMER.	Bluefields and English Bank,	1848		53		53	53		53	53	53	
DANISH WEST INDIES.												
ST. THOMAS.	New Herrnhut,	1732	231	81	287	599		319	918			
	Niesky,	1753	384	90	391	865		234	1,099			
	Town of St. Thomas,	1843	123	24	95	242		18	260			
ST. CROIX.	Friedensthal,	1754	716	128	437	1,281	6,758	612	1,893	9,776	9,776	9,776 Negroes.
	Friedensberg,	1771	490	56	436	982		645	1,627			
	Friedensfeld,	1804	750	237	609	1,596		725	2,321			
ST. JAN.	Bethany,	1754	157	37	167	361		167	528			
	Emmaus,	1782	307	84	441	832		298	1,130			

BRITISH WEST INDIES.												
JAMAICA.	Fairfield,	1823	604	99	560	1,263		306	1,569			
	New Eden,	1812	297	71	350	718		159	877			
	Irwin Hill,	1815	181	43	309	533		159	692			
	New Carmel,	1827	426	143	650	1,219		349	1,568			
	New Bethlehem,	1833	244	48	300	592		111	703			
	New Fulneck,	1830	380	70	550	1,000		237	1,237			
	New Nazareth,	1838	246	33	330	609	10,486	159	768	12,952		
	Beaufort,	1834	204	41	290	525		140	675			
	New Hope,	1838	254	110	450	814		178	992			
	Litiz,	1839	340	52	480	872		102	974			
	Bethany,	1835	404	85	577	1,066		304	1,370			
	Bethabara,	1840	350	62	300	712		119	831			
	Springfield,	1848	197	65	291	558		143	696			
ANTIGUA.	St. John's, with Five Islands, and Green Bay,	1756	1,417	194	700	2,311		198	2,509			
	Gracehill,	1774	601	165	475	1,241		48	1 289			
	Gracebay,	1797	334	50	300	684		59	743			
	Cedar Hall,	1822	566	138	567	1,271	7,372	168	1,439	8,048	29,376	60,497 Negroes.
	Newfield,	1817	285	25	226	536		51	587			
	Lebanon,	1838	370	101	300	771		103	874			
	Gracefield,	1840	262	34	262	558		49	607			
ST. KITT'S.	Basseterre,	1777	498	139	585	1,222		338	1,560			
	Bethesda,	1820	293	72	373	738	2,750	145	883	3,461		
	Estridge,	1845	202	89	100	481		137	618			
	Bethel,	1832	132	57	120	309		91	400			
BARBADOES.	Bridgetown,	1836	117	29	82	228		121	349			
	Sharon,	1767	461	98	673	1,282	2,328	161	1,393	2,839		
	Mount Tabor,	1825	199	86	277	562		152	714			
	Clifton Hill,	1841	88	18	200	306		77	383			
TOBAGO.	Montgomery,	1827	521	147	611	1,219	1,745	205	1,484	2,076		
	Moriah,	1842	214	62	190	466		126	592			

PROVINCES AND STATIONS.	Date of Establishment.	Communicants.	Baptized Adults.	Baptized Children.	Total in Church Fellowship.	Total in each Island or Colony.	Candidates for Baptism, New People, and Excluded.	Total under Instruction in the Stations.	Total in each Island or Colony.	Total under the several Governments.	NATIONAL NUMBERS.
SOUTH AMERICA.											
SURINAM. Paramaribo,	1776	1,621	1,348	850	3,819		1,683	5,502			
Rust-en Werk,	1845	51	201	96	348		465	813			
Liliendal,	1849	102	480	277	859		547	1,406			
Annazorg,	1849	80	421	362	863		999	1,862			
Charlottenberg,	1835	156	1,416	515	2,087	11,109	3,735	5,822	21,345	21,345	21,345 Negroes.
Catherine Sophia,	1849	66	395	202	663		471	1,134			
Hanover,		132	1,141	376	1,649		2,122	3,771			
Salem,	1840	205	252	248	705		185	890			
Bambey,	1841	27	29	60	116		29	145			
SOUTH AFRICA.											
Genadendal,	1792	952	440	1,155	2,547		593	3,140			
Mamre (in Groenekloof),	1808	373	236	563	1,172		106	1,278			
Robben Island,	1823	17	24	2	43		44	87			
Elim,	1824	356	192	463	1,011	5,482	261	1,272	7,037	7,037	7,037 Hottentots, &c.
Enon,	1818	73	48	125	246		49	295			
Clarkson,	1839	79	32	124	235		135	370			
Shiloh, Hottentots,	1828	36	30	110	176		32	208			
Shiloh, Tambookies,		21	17	14	52		335	387			
AUSTRALIA.											
Lake Boga,	1849										
Totals,		19,583	10,607	21,245	51,435		19,912	71,347	71,347	71,347	

Of the above gross amount, there are—

Subjects of the British Crown,	Negroes, &c.,	29,376	
	Indians,	205	
	Hottentots, &c.,	7,037	
	Esquimaux,	1,221	
			37,839
Crown of Denmark,	Negroes, &c.,	9,776	
	Greenlanders,	2,053	
			11,829
Crown of Holland,	Negroes, &c.,		21,345
Residing in the United States,	Indians,		281
" on the Mosquito Coast,	Indians, &c.,		53
			71,347
Total, about the middle of 1855,			71,060
Increase,			287

SUMMARY.

70 Stations,	300 Missionaries.
Last year, 68 Stations,	295 Missionaries.
Increase, 2 Stations,	5 Missionaries.

During the year, 23 missionaries retired, 6 died, and 32 were called into active service.

But the Lot was the source also of more domestic appeals.

Matrimonial projects were confirmed or negatived by its decision.

If a brother wanted a wife, he made his want known to his minister or the Conference, by whom—naming an helpmate—the question was submitted to God in the Lot; if the answer was yea, it was well; if nay, another was proposed. But even before this, Abraham did no less, having obtained a wife for his son by submitting the whole matter to the Lord, as, in Genesis 24:14, his servant prayeth, "And let it come to pass that the damsel, to whom I shall say, Let down thy pitcher, I pray thee, that I may drink, and she shall say, Drink, and I will give thy camels drink also, let the same be she that thou hast appointed for thy servant Isaac."

It has often happened that the parties had never seen each other, but were only known by reputation.

America has thus joined Germany, and Germany has been linked to the West Indies, whilst England and Greenland have kissed each other by proxical contract.

Faith sanctified the union; for it is a remarkable fact, that, however strange this mode of the connubial tie may appear to the world, it is no less true, that when enacted in the spirit of truthful faith, an unhappy union was an anomaly.

Marriage was not a carnal fancy: what God hath put together, was their motto, and to Him they appealed for the union; neither was it a distinction by birth, blood, or education; but the Lord God said, "It is not good that the man should be alone: I will make him an help meet for him;" the man therefore sought an help meet, for his requirements, through the oracle, at the time appointed by the Church. Neither was the glitter of wealth the beacon of a matrimonial harbor; the mind's eye, lit by purity of thought, rested on faith, for an answer by the Lot, and happy were the results.

"Be ye clean, that bear the vessels of the Lord." (Isaiah, 52 : 11.)

The Lot was a vessel of the Lord, and always committed to holy hands.

Its burden was a subject of devout prayer, under the especial promise of our Saviour, that where two or three are gathered together in my name, there am I in the midst of them. (Matthew, 18 : 20.)

Being administered by three senior clergy, it could not err, so long as theirs was the "prayer of faith;" for the promises of God are yea and amen, and "the testimony of the Lord is sure, making wise the simple." (Psalm 19 : 7.)

They, therefore, laying aside all self or selfish motives, appealed to that fountain of wisdom, that only could beautify their simplicity, and it did so.

It, however, never was intended as an ordinary mantle for the covering of responsibility, nor were common-sense matters exonerated by its use, but in all important matters where sound judgment was at fault.

The Lot was the vessel that bore them to and from the Throne of Grace, directed in their course by the sure mercies of David.

"Incline your ear, and come unto me; hear and your soul shall live, and I will make an everlasting covenant with you, even the sure mercies of David." (Isaiah, 55 : 3.)

Thus, based upon Holy Writ, the Lot was an unerring guide, and proof upon proof of its perfect issues exist even now throughout the world; but it was their *Moses*, "on the top of the hill," so long as "Aaron and Hur" held up his hands, the Israelites prevailed. (See Exodus, 17 : 12.) And so long as the Church supported this standard, it never failed.

But alas, the "Spirit of the Age," has long been controverting the utility of the privilege, has fought it to the hilt, and is even now treading upon its shades, as they yield to the wisdom or the wanderings of refined Christianity. And why this? If it was good and true then, what has reduced its value now? The exercise of faith is no less important now than it was then, nor has our need of asking in aught diminished.

The refinement of the age has certainly not refined Christianity to such perfection as to need no guide; nor has the wisdom of man yet reached the heavens, to counsel the angels.

Childlike simplicity is no less a saving virtue now, than when our Saviour said, "Except ye be converted, and become as little children, ye shall not enter into the kingdom of heaven." (Matt. 18 : 3.) But humility seems to be weighed in the balance, "and is found wanting."

Jesus Christ, the same yesterday, to-day, and forever, the same source of every good and perfect gift, to be approached in the same manner, by faith, humility, and childlike simplicity; and yet, the Church that once enjoyed the full privilege of especial assurance of safeguard, guided to extensive growth, prospered for its simplicity, and was "blessed in its deed," has been compromising its spiritual might for an *ad libitum* chance of its own judgment.

It was obligatory on members of the Church to marry

by the Lot; and if they would not, they were excluded, and in the place congregations were compelled to leave.

This requirement was annulled some forty years ago, and the rule applied to ministers only; and this now is compromised for the taste, the fancy, or the judgment even of the minister.

Congregations, seeing this dereliction of the fathers, claim the right of choice of a pastor; and the Lot to them is of none effect. And now, extreme necessity only reserves the use of the Lot for its direction. What that *extreme* may dwindle to, ten more years will show; for the children of this world are wiser in their generation than the children of light.

This tie of perfection is certainly passing rapidly into nonenity; and the simple abiding faith of the early fathers is merging into the shamefacedness of worldly considerations. I do not mean to say that the Church is less sound in doctrines, principles, or faith, but she certainly has yielded this leading point—so faithful in all its acts—to specious arguments of doubtful issues, and is taking an unnecessary round. "The fervent effectual prayer of a righteous man availeth much." And the Lot *was* a faithful messenger, if faithfully used, to and from the heavenly court of appeal.

Far be it from me to cast undeserved odium upon my spiritual mother; or to soil her escutcheons with "untempered mortar," nay, rather would I be a Ham, or a Japheth, with my back to her foibles, and drop a veil of oblivion over the startling evidences of her dereliction.

But history has claims to all of the past, and justice to the manes of our fathers belongs to the future. St. Paul says, 3 Philippians, 16, 17, "Nevertheless, whereto we have already attained, let us walk by the same rule, let us mind the same thing." "Brethren, be followers together of me, and mark them which walk, as ye have us for examples."

Seeing, then, that the present *régime* has swallowed down and is hiding the example of our fathers; dimming, if not extinguishing, a light that not only shone far and wide, but emitted from its rays a warm and fructifying influence; the bemoaning of Job (29th chapter) seems like a spontaneous flow of lamentation, at the loss or compromise of the blessings of our youth. "Oh that I were as in months past, as in the days when God preserved me!" "When his candle shined upon my head, and when, by his light, I walked through darkness." "As I was in the days of my youth, when the secret of God was upon my tabernacle."

It is much to be feared, that such will be the bemoanings of ours, or any other Church, that sinks its primitive, faith-abiding simplicity in the uncertain experiments of progression, compromising quality for quantity.

CHAPTER XXII.

Feasts and Fasts.

The Church had its feasts and its fasts, and they were duly observed.

Christmas, Easter, Epiphany, Ascension Day, Whitsuntide, and the several Memorial Days of the Church, were ecclesiological feast days; and Ash Wednesday to Easter Sunday, were included as, commonly called, fast days, or a chastened mode of life, for and during the forty days of Lent.

The feast of Shrove Tuesday, and the very savory odor of its pancakes and doughnuts, was but too suddenly merged in the restrictive requirement of Ash Wednesday, which, as well as Good Friday, in the immediate atmosphere of my appetital privileges, was redolent of fish; to my palate, a most unsavory service, and a very chastening to my youthful cravings.

These days were generally marked more literally as fasts, than the others of the Lent season; though temperance in all things, and at all times, was a respected and observed motto of the Moravians.

THE CHRISTMAS FESTIVAL.

The celebration of the Birth of Christ is, and ever has been, a high and holy time in the Church, and commences its religious services on the evening before Christmas Day.

These Christmas Eve services are at once imposing and inspiring, as well from the fact itself, as from the portrait of the scene of his birth, and its attendant circumstances, as set forth in the history of that great event; rendered even more impressive by the occasional introduction of anthems of praise, and other devotional melody, opening to the spiritual eye the Bethlehem Manger; and, like the shepherds by the star, leading the congregation to the joyful reality of the Nativity of the promised Redeemer; offering the incense of adorative salutation in melodious strains of

"Welcome, thou source of every good,
O Jesus, King of Glory.
Welcome, thrice welcome, Lamb of God,
To this world transitory.

"In grateful hymns thy name we'll praise,
With heart and voice throughout our days,
For thy blest incarnation,
Procured our salvation."

And lighting up the vista to the radii, from the infant brow of the new-born King; whilst

"Arise my spirit! Bless the day,
Whereon the age's Sire
A child became; thy homage pay,
Receive him with desire.
This is the night in which he came,
Was born, and put on human frame,
Us sinners to deliver,
From sin and death forever,"

was a very appropriate exordium, from the hearts of the

congregation, as they rendered "the calves of their lips," and pledged their brotherly affection in the participation of the religious enjoyment of the proffered and passing love-feast.

CHRISTMAS DAY.

The order of services on this day was the usual and regular Sunday worship, saving the special application of the history of the Nativity of our Saviour.

SECOND CHRISTMAS DAY.

The day after Christmas was so called, and so appropriated.

There was Divine service and a sermon in the morning; and in the afternoon the children had their annual love-feast; said their verses, answered questions, and listened attentively to the admonitory exordium of their venerable pastor.

This service was indelible in impression on the youthful mind; and any that ever were participants of its offerings, temporal and spiritual, must ever remember the joyful gathering, and the sunny smiles of a Second Christmas Day in the Moravian Church.

The congregation being small, the children were few. Twelve years and under, was the compass of the privilege of this enjoyment. Two benches on either side, in front of the minister's table, the girls to the right, and the boys to the left, contained the gathering; whilst mothers and nurses, supporting the gazing and wondering infant, reaching, or perhaps fretting for the passing cake, were seated on the wall benches, in front of the youth, who were restive for the kindly evidence of the love of their spiritual fathers, casting a wistful eye to the entrance from the parsonage, even until the click of the latch betokened the approaching bounty.

Two male and two female chapel servants, bearing trays of half-pint cups, evaporating savory fumes of chocolate, and two baskets, redolent of the odor of light cake, were soon relieved of their burden as they kissed the lips that greeted their issues, whilst unplied hands awaited the return of the palatable supply of their share. This course was followed by a gingerbread horse, or infant-shaped, to each child, and with it a book, of some eight or ten pages, with mottled pasteboard cover, not a cheap book, but of duodecimo size, containing hymns touching the Nativity, and after this a printed half sheet, with a special hymn or ode, to be said, or sung, on the next ensuing Christmas. The book was unpictured, but so neatly bound as to render it worthy of their particular care, and it was always produced, and said at the call of the minister, on that day.

THE PASSION WEEK.

The fundamental principle of our Holy Religion is, "Christ and Him Crucified," the Rock of our Salvation, and the Polar Star of all our hopes.

Everything connected with this important event, important to every soul of man, is, as "wisdom justified of all her children," the Life of Light to poor, fallen human nature. And although it be the theme of every Christian Church, as from the days of the Apostles, "so we preach, and so ye believed;" yet to make this more than a mere *historical* belief, the shameful trial of our Saviour, and the dismal avenues of his travel from Gethsemane to Golgotha, are of too much importance to that godly sorrow, which "worketh repentance," to pass with the mere currency of the ordinary Sabbath's offering.

With this view, the Moravian Church adopted, as they thought, and as we indorse, a more active and impressive avenue to the *practised* faith of its members.

The Passion of our Saviour is, therefore, annually memorialized by a succession of evening meetings, from Palm Sunday evening to the Burial on Good Friday evening.

They differ from their brethren of the Church of England, not only in the *form* of presenting the history, but also in the *manner* of conducting the service.

"The Acts of the Days of the Son of Man, from the Passion Week to His Ascension," are a compend of the Four Gospels, and harmonize the whole into a regular narrative, connecting his sayings and doings from day to day for that week.

A separate service, is, therefore, held on every evening of the week, beginning with Palm Sunday, detailing the acts of that day.

The first meeting is opened by prayer and an illustrative address from the minister. The reading is relieved of the *semblance* of monotony by the introduction of a suitable verse or hymn at different points of the narrative, aided in solemnity, and deepening the impressiveness of the scene, as its godlike majesty yields to the severity and vengeance of human depravity.

Maunday, or Mandate Thursday, so called from the institution of the Last Supper, on that day, and the command of our Saviour to his disciples thus to commemorate him, is particularly solemnized by an implicit obedience to, and observance of, the memorial and the injunction.

To this end, the afternoon of that day is appropriated to this service, the formula being the same as on the stated meetings for that purpose; but the preceding development of the increasing sufferings of Christ, having imbued the mind with a solemnity, arising from the continuous review of his painful times, the soul is the more susceptible of, and certainly does enjoy the spiritual life presented and intended by the Holy Offering. And if there can be any difference in solemnity in the administration of the Lord's Supper, it is on this special occasion, as on bended knee the participants hymn their faith and their acknowledgments. They melt and mingle their heart's effusions in poetic strains, thus:

"Act, full of Godlike majesty,
O Love's abyss, I am lost in thee,
O mystery all our thoughts surpassing,
Now all our wants are well supplied;
And we show forth that Jesus died
As oft as we enjoy this blessing."

In the evening, the acts of Thursday are continued and finished.

The high priestly prayer being a part of this service, is read, the congregation standing; and as the narrative proceeds, and leads the mind to the garden of Gethsemane, and the Hail, Master! is followed by a treacherous kiss, the heart, prepared for confession and supplication, the devout and prayerful outpouring from the sacred desk reaches the kindred spirit of the bowed assemblage, who breathe their heartful response in one of Zinzendorff's most happy conceptions, thus set forth:

> "Most Holy Lord and God,
> Holy, almighty God,
> Holy and most merciful Saviour,
> Thou eternal God,
> Bless thy congregation.
> Through thy sufferings, death, and blood,
> Have mercy, O Lord."

The nature and import of this part of the history, the vocal harmony of chastened thought combined with the mellow tones of the organ, all mingle with the spiritual might of the ministerial effort, and heart answers to heart with tearful evidences of a renewed impression of its own unworthiness, and the agonizing sacrifice for its redemption.*

GOOD FRIDAY.

The solemnities of this day are pursued in the same manner as those preceding, varying only in the adaptation of the hymn or verse, as the account of the trial, the condemnation, and the crucifixion progresses.

The forenoon of the day was appropriated to this service, and the afternoon to the regular Divine service and a sermon.

Good Friday is a high and a holy day in the Church, and is held especially sacred to the memory of the agonizing sufferings of Christ.

In the evening, the narrative is concluded with the

* This order of service has been reversed; the Communion being administered in the evening instead of the afternoon, and reading in the afternoon for the accommodation of the communicant members.

details of the descent from the cross, and the burial, under the liberal and kindly sympathies of Joseph of Arimathea; but as the narrative is short, it partakes more of a liturgical service, and deepens in interest as hymn adds to hymn the heartfelt sympathies, working a "godly sorrow" in the subjects of that wrath that cost so great a sacrifice to appease. This observance from first to last is by no means wrought in fancy. Its effect upon the soul is indescribable, and its influence upon spiritual growth is worthy of any sacrifice to obtain.

Where the Spirit of God is so earnestly and so continuously invoked, it comes in virtue of the promise, "Ask, and ye shall receive," and illumines the halo of its congenial atmosphere, increasing faith, and in a great measure realizing the pursuit of their souls. They, therefore, in heart and voice, hymn the life of their faith in the melodious offerings of their souls.

"Though we can't see our Saviour
With these, our mortal eyes,
Our Faith, which tastes his favor,
The want of sight supplies.
Our hearts can feel him near,
So that to us 'tis clear,
His presence is as certain
As if we saw him here."

This closes the penitential services of the season of Lent, and leaves an impression that is not easily obliterated.

EASTER DAY.

The momentous period of the resurrection is at hand, the sepulchre has had its charge, the stone sealed, and the watch had been set.

"If Christ be not risen, then is our preaching vain, and your faith is also vain;" thus saith St. Paul, 1 Corinth. 15 : 14, and so we believe; and in virtue of our faith, the resurrection is celebrated, at early dawn of the day, with full purpose of heart, to the praise and glory of God.

This service opens at five o'clock in the morning of Easter Sunday.

The organ announces the joyous victory, with all its powers.

The minister enters, the organ ceases, the congregation rise, whilst the minister makes the declaration in audible tone.

"The Lord is risen, the Lord is risen indeed." Then follows the choral of adorative rejoicing.

> "Hail, all hail, victorious Lord and Saviour,
> Thou hast burst the bonds of death;
> Grant us as to Mary, that great favor,
> To embrace thy feet in faith.
> Thou hast in our stead the cross endured,
> And for us eternal life procured;
> Joyful we, with one accord,
> Hail Thee, as our risen Lord."

The history of the great event then follows; after which, the "Easter Morning Litany" is most impressively read by the minister, and as impressively responded to; and as the creed or faith of the Church is developed, and paragraph succeeds paragraph, a short stanza of music lights up the service as it nears its conclusion. The whole service ends with the following confirmation of the faith of the Church.

> "Christ is risen from the dead.
> Thou shalt rise, too, saith my Saviour;

Of what should I be afraid,
I with him shall live forever.
Can the head forsake its limb,
And not draw me unto him?

"No, my soul, he cannot leave:
This, this is my consolation;
And my body in the grave
Rests in hope and expectation,
That this mortal flesh shall see,
Incorruptibility."

Hard must be the heart and obstinate the sensibilities that can resist the influence of such a delineation of the merits of the life, sufferings, and death of the Redeemer, and no less obtuse the soul, that cannot swell a grateful lay, at the conquest in His resurrection from the dead.

The mode and character of this review is graphic, and calculated to carry the soul back to the scene of the original facts, and imbue it with a holy certainty, ineffaceable by time, sense, or infidelity.

And such is the effect, evidenced firstly by the extensive gathering.

Secondly. By the strict attention to the subject before them. And,

Thirdly. By the decided influence upon them, as sincere worshippers of Jesus Christ.

The depiction of the resurrection is rendered even more interesting in the town or country congregations, where, after reading the history in the church, the whole congregation proceed in form to the burial-ground, preceded by a band of trombones, who, with choral harmony, lead them to the brow of the hill, and there, after the solemn voice of the Easter Morning Litany, swell the welkin with bursts of harmonious rejoicing, at the conquest of Christ over sin, death, hell, and the grave.

This ceremony, lit by the early dawn, and even gilt as the sun peeps over the horizon, at the sacred memorabilia, as if to hallow the offering of adoration, is even more interesting and impressive in the country than in the city congregations.

There, from the sepulchres of those who await a "glorious resurrection to the life of the world to come, "He who is the resurrection and the life is announced as having burst the tomb, and "led captivity captive;" and thence the spiritual greeting of Him, who, as on that eventful morn, fulfilled all prophecy concerning himself, and thence too the confession of faith, and the grateful outpourings of a worshipping assembly.

The place, the time of day, the liturgical service, the union of heart and soul, filling the atmosphere with the poetical melody of their affections, can never fail to make an indelible impression upon every participant in this beautiful service.

EASTER MONDAY.

The ecclesiological year closes with the Easter holidays, and on the evening of Easter Monday, after reading of our Saviour's appearance and walk with two of his disciples to Emmaus, &c. &c., a love-feast was distributed, and an account of the finances, arising from various contributions throughout the year, as well as a detail of the expenditures, was submitted to the congregation, who always passed the *exposé* without a dissenting voice.

This association, however, being found inconvenient,

and perhaps rather incongruous, the financial affairs have been separated, and anticipated earlier in the year. And the evening of Easter Monday is exclusively observed as a meeting for religious worship, consummating the whole in a love-feast, which the next chapter will more fully explain.

CHAPTER XXIII.

The Agapæ, or Love-feasts.

THE antiquity and practice of keeping love-feasts as a religious ceremonial, having Holy Writ for its basis, has been continued from the earliest date of Moravianism; not only by the Moravians, but by several other Christian denominations, differing, however, in manner and in matter.

The "Dunkers" observed it more as a "feast of charity" or benevolence, and hence, more apostolically than some of the other observers of the custom. They have meat, potatoes, soup, &c. &c., and feed their poor as an act of loving kindness.

The Methodists serve bread and water; whilst the Moravians serve coffee, in some places, and chocolate and cake in others; both as a test of love and unity in their congregations, and not as a general hunger-appeasing feast.

Whatever the material may be, the spirit is the same, though the modern mode, or dispensation, is evidently a compromise of the ancient; but, as then, so now, it is regarded as a religious observance.

Love feasts, and the "kiss of peace," were originally connected with the Holy Communion, and even in the present century, was so ordered in the town congregations of the Moravian Church, where also they were, and are yet, more frequent than in the city churches; memorial days, and choir festivals, being there more particularly observed than here, saving that the facilities of retirement protect the participants from the gaze and intrusion of idle curiosity.

Under a different *régime*, after the times when the Apostles "had all things in common," the love-feast was substituted.

St. Chrysostom says, "Upon certain days, after partaking of the Lord's Supper, they met at a common table, the rich bringing provisions, and the poor who had nothing, being invited." The spirit is still the same, since the poor members or worshippers in the Society, are always invited, without the expectation of "any pecuniary return."

In the early time of this church, the love-feasts were paid for by contributions of the more able members; the expense being small, one member sometimes, and again at others some two, three, four, and even six, liquidated the charge.

In more modern times, and even now, the expense is defrayed by a general collection after service, at which those who choose, or are able, may contribute.

The stated times for these love-feasts, in this church, were Christmas Eve, second Christmas Day, New Year's Eve, and Easter Monday evening.

But, in addition to these, a visit by the Bishop, or any other official of the Church, was always welcomed with a congregational love-feast.

It also aided the solemnities of the farewell ceremonies of a departing pastor, and greeted his successor with loving kindness; whilst the congregation, giving wings to their supplications, appealed to the throne of grace, from the melody of their hearts.

"Lord Jesus, for our call of grace,
To praise thy name in fellowship,
We're humbly met before thy face,
And in thy presence love-feast keep.
Shed on our hearts thy love abroad,
Thy Spirit's unction now impart.
Grant we may all, O Lamb of God,
In thee be truly one in heart."

These, and other like sentiments, in like manner, gave a spiritual zest to the temporal ceremonial.

The discipline was exacting upon the members of this association.

If a brother or sister was at variance with others of the Church, they were required to be "first reconciled, and then come and offer their gift;" and if they could not settle their difference amicably, a reference to the pastor generally softened their asperity, and equalized a spirit of forgiveness; but if this failed—which, however, seldom happened—the dissenting parties could not be admitted.

"Let the peace of God rule in your hearts, to the which, also, ye are called in one body," was an injunction well ordered, and well observed in the pristine discipline of this Church.

The march of improvement had not yet refined Christian simplicity, nor led its purity to the shrine of etiquette and formality.

Doubtless, there were crooked disciples, too, in those days; but certainly they were "few, and far between;"

but great would be the pen that could trace all the virtues of our fathers in the present generation!

Truly, the spirit of the age does not seem to have done much for the apostolic and humble bearing of the early fathers of the Church.

The Moravian Church is well known; as well for its distinctive features as for its missionary spirit and labors; and the continuance of its wholesome practices must, or ought to be, ever and anon, not only religious, but a profitable inheritance from the early fathers.

For although the religious peculiarities of the Church were neither rubrical nor doctrinal, they were all drawn from Scripture, and are ably supported, as well by precept as by example; and were profitable, as well for doctrine as for "reproof, correction, and instruction in righteousness, that the man of God might be perfect, thoroughly furnished unto all good works."

It is, therefore, a pleasurable association with the spirit of our fathers, to memorialize them and their happy and pious efforts, as we yet meet,

"And in God's presence, love-feast keep."

Unavoidable and untoward circumstances, chargeable to the general march of improvement, however, or the refinement of the age, have limited the privilege in our city churches to the periods already laid down; and Christmas afternoon, New Year's Eve, and Easter Monday evening, are still memorialized by the holy keeping of a congregational love-feast.

A MORAVIAN SISTER IN COSTUME.

CHAPTER XXIV.

Dress, Address, and Manners of the Early Moravians.

"Let your moderation be known to all men," though general in its application, may be rendered specific in its results.

That the Moravians were a plain, unassuming people, is evident from the still existing relics of their simplicity, a cardinal virtue, obnoxious to fashion, forbidding to vain show, but fraternizing with economy, and harmonizing with their Christian profession.

Their apparel, therefore, was unstudied, except in cleanliness, and their taste chastened by disciplined judgment. The strait, unlapelled, dark brown coat, the broad-brimmed, low-crowned hat, the knee-buckled small clothes, the broad, round-toed shoe, were consistent characteristics of a Moravian brother; whilst the plain drab or black silk bonnet, the three-cornered white kerchief, the plain silk gown (Sunday dress), the comfortable hood-finished cloak, the "stuff" shoe, for comfort and convenience, were the sisters' concession to St. Peter's advice, "whose adorning, let it not be that outward adorning of plaiting the hair, and wearing of gold, or putting on of apparel."

Their manners were bland, courteous, and winning. Whilst the essence of their souls illumined their brow, and the lustre of their countenance reflected the harmony of their peace-imbued hearts, their address was the growth of our Saviour's planting, who said to his disciples, "One is your Master, even Christ, and all ye are *brethren*;" and watered by St. Paul, "For both he that sanctifieth and they who are sanctified, are all of one; for which cause, he is not ashamed to call them *brethren*."

The salutation, therefore, was "Brother," to brother, and "Sister," to sister; and this custom continued inviolate, till within the last thirty-seven years, since 1820 witnessed the fractional falling off of the ties that bound heart to heart, in the bond of brotherly friendship. A "Mister," or a "Mistress," was not known, and the appellation would have called up a blush and a frown upon the recipient of such refinement. Like their Master, they were not ashamed to call each other brethren.

The wedge of waywardness, once entered, made a chasm, difficult, if ever, to be reunited, and worst of all, the evil began at the fountain head.

Fashion paid its respects to Bethlehem, and Bethlehem in courtesy accepted, and vied in the compliment; and some were ashamed or thought it too old-fashioned, and perhaps too simple, to say, "*Brother*," and even amongst themselves, "Mister," seemed to sound more dignified.

Without boasting, Philadelphia was, and is even yet, more tenacious of its early education, impression, and conviction.

"Rend your hearts, and not your garments," was the well-observed manners in cases of death.

It was a privilege and a *principle* of the Church to eschew outward mourning for a deceased relative, of any grade, and the sable habiliment was never offered to deepen the shade of a sorrowing heart, till early in the present century, when Fashion offered its services, and the full-craped hat presented its claims to human sympathy. Philadelphia had not yet advanced in *this* refinement.

A brother from here, on a visit to Bethlehem, seeing one pass in the sable hue of sorrow, said to the writer of this, "There goes one dissatisfied with God's providence."

Grief, of course, could not be forbidden nor suppressed, but it might be chastened; the community was instructed first, to believe that the departed were gone home; and, therefore, secondly, "not to grieve as they that are without hope." If any insignia of bereavement *was* adopted, it was a white ribbon on a sister's bonnet; but the brother continued his usual dress; but, even now, the fountain-head of example can boast of more shades of sorrow than its Philadelphia charge.

There was a time when peace encircled our borders, and its influence sat smiling upon the countenances of the inhabitants of our little Zion; when a brother could answer the inquiry after his well-being, "*kind vergnügt*," happy as a child. Alas! alas! for the irrevocable distance of the things that were!

What is gained by the novelties of the day, in exchange for the more immediate influence of a pure spirit, unchecked by the flitting clouds of worldly interference? What is gained by the circuitous route to that "holiness, without which no man shall see God?"

Our Saviour said, "Except ye become as a little child," &c.; our kindly ecclesiological patron set the example, and taught childlike simplicity; but, brethren, where are we now? There *is* such a thing as keeping up wholesome discipline.

The Society of Friends, as a body, have deviated less than the Moravians from their original simplicity; their plain dress yet qualifies their plainness of speech; whilst their calm and moral bearing marks their distinctive character, and presents a consistency worthy of emulation.

That there may be, and doubtless are, crooked disciples amongst them, is not to be disputed; but, if they become too knotty, and will not be straightened, their membership is forfeited.

Without controversy, it may be asserted that a Quaker in black would certainly be a curiosity; nor is it common for them to disparage their profession by a compromise, even of their plain language. Differing from them, as we do, in our religious views, they are justly entitled to the respect and the protection of the world, for their chastening influence, and promotion of the peace of the places wherein they dwell; and this being conceded, the wonder cannot be wondered at, that others, who had built upon the same foundation, and were originally quite as well taught and disciplined, could not do likewise. "Brethren, these things ought not so to be."

CHAPTER XXV.

The Music and its Application—Church Choirs—Objections, &c.

It will not be necessary to show up the origin, or prove the use of instrumental music in the Church, seeing that, from Genesis to Revelations, precept and example fully set it forth, as a medium to elevate the soul, or chasten the senses, as occasion might require.

In this Church, the science of music has ever been an appendage to the education of its ministers, and few there are, who are not able themselves to perform the services, or consistently advise with the officers and members of that department.

This being the case, beside the cardinal point of a strictly religious application of its powers, it has been ever guarded as a sacred avenue to the heart, and a medium of inspiration to "the praise and glory of God." Light or frivolous exhibitions of talent, taste, or fancy on the organ, were positively forbidden, and, as heretofore noted, silence was commanded and enforced for any infraction of the order.

Anthems were only allowed on special occasions, and they were always in point of praise, prayer, or supplication.

The tunes principally used were collated and published by the Rev. C. Gregor, in Germany, entitled, "Choral

Buch, enthaltend alle zu dem Gesangbuch der Evangelischen Brüdergemeinen vom Jahr 1778, Gehorige Melodien: Leipsig, 1784."

These tunes were set in the tenor cleff and written in semibreves, and figured for thorough bass. They are productions of the best masters, and are religious emanations from the very *soul* of the *science* of music.

They were not named, but numbered, and 9, 10, 15, 22, 26, or any other number in the tune book, was as familiar to the organist as Meer, Hotham, or any other cognomen to modern productions.

But they were also set to particular hymns, and the first line of almost any one of them, was sufficient indication of the melody to follow.

To this the congregations were educated by practice, aided by a strict adhesion to their own tunes, so that in Labrador, or Ireland, a Moravian would know his immediate brethren, in a Church service, although till then a stranger in a strange land.

The organ has long been the leading patron of the sacred melody, not, however, as a fancy accompaniment, but as a *support* to the congregational harmony, which else, in singing many verses, is apt to sink, and thus produce discord.

But the organist was expected to enter into the spirit of his office, and to be actuated by a devotional spirit, as he led the hymning assembly to praise or petition.

The Rev. Christian Ignatius Latrobe, in his Preface to his extract of the original tune book, says:

"There is scarcely a person in the Church who more easily exposes his inattention and want of true devotion, than the organist; nor is it to be wondered at, that sincere and devout people conceive a musical instrument improper in a church, because they have never heard it *properly* used."

What would Brother Latrobe say, were he a worshipper in some churches of the present day, where snatches of song, operatic flirts, and unfledged, fanciful jets of disconnected apologies for ideas, are dealt out boldly, and most self-complacently palmed upon a congregation to amuse, instead of edify, corrupting taste and good manners, and in a great measure "making the Word of God of none effect."

The organist in this church has a respectable standing, and is not viewed as a mere underling. His business being to assist in the devotion, he works hand in hand with the minister; by which intercourse, advised of the nature of the subject to be presented, either by direct communication or the character of the hymns prescribed in advance, harmonizes his sentiments, and gives religiously, or at least respectfully, the shades or the lights that are to come from the sacred desk.

The instrumental music, of which this Church is nowhere sparse, was neither intended nor allowed as a diversion or an amusement in the interim of the service; but if as accompaniment, they were subdued to sacred requirements; if as voluntaries, solemnization of the waiting assemblage was incumbent upon them; and if as for interludes, a befitting short modulation, leading the mind soberly onward to the successive sentiment of the hymn before them; whilst if for festivals, they might shout their thanks in noble strains, and "make a joyful noise," or, joined by sonorous trombones, search the welkin for an echo of praise to the ever adorable Trinity; but in all cases, and at all times, everything was done "decently and in order."

In the congregational places, various musical instruments are in use, but in this, there was but one appendage to the organ, and that only occasionally.

A single brother, of ancient date, had a penchant for "stringed instruments;"—the violin was his hobby, and church music his beau ideal of its enjoyment.

The importance of this old gentleman was no mean consideration, and the choir music, or anthems, were deemed incomplete without the vibrating evidence of his presence, or the audible pizzicato of his A, to harmonize with the organ.

He sat "otium cum dignitate," at the side of the organ, with his stand before him, lit up by a tallow candle, in a broad-bottomed candle-stick, supported by a board jutting from the square of his triangular desk, and balanced by a four-pound weight, at the other end; to all which a twitch of the risibles was scarcely repressible, especially when his audible whisper to the organist, for his A, and the consequent pizzicato of his string, drew the attention of the quiet audience, to witness the eager ear, to catch the tone as he drew the bow to prove his perfect fifth.

The elder brethren, compassionating his infirmity, rubbed their ears, to mitigate the pain and compromise the penalty.

This extra, however, was confined to the winter and spring, which happened to include the festivals; but the congregation was favored, *nolens volens*, with the stringy streak in the choral services, during the whole of the patronizing sojourn of this venerable amateur; and, although he muted the bridge of his "braach," as he most significantly called it, a viola or tenor, he could not forego the gratification of satisfying himself by a stroke from heel to tip of his bow, that he had enriched the harmony, and perfected the combined efforts of the organist and his choir.

The vocal department was sustained generally by boys, of from ten to thirteen years of age, of which the writer had the honor of being one; and we were taught to venerate our calling, and to sing with devotional demeanor and full purpose of heart, to the praise and glory of God. We, of course, sang by rote more than by note, and were drilled some time in advance of the respective services; but the exemplary deportment of our pious organist not only forbade levity, but imbued us with the reverence due to the solemnity of the place and the purpose; and when, for the Christmas festival, we sang,

> "Our Saviour's birth and bitter passion,
> Cause everlasting jubilation,
> For his dear congregation,
> Hallelujah!"

we were made to understand it. Or, when,

> "Hark, the herald angels sing,
> Glory to the new-born King;
> Peace on earth and mercy mild,
> God and sinners reconciled.
> Joyful all ye nations rise,
> Join the triumph of the skies;
> With the angelic hosts proclaim,
> Christ is born in Bethlehem,

flowed from our lips, our sensibilities responded, from our hearts, a corresponding influence to inspire the sacred song.

There was no proxical worship of any kind, nor aught

of exhibition of fancy, taste, or skill. "We want no embellishment," said our sober organist, when, on one occasion—and only one—one of us perpetrated an unbidden turn; simply he played, and simply we must sing.

In after-time, some two or three girls were admitted to the choir; but we were kept apart by our guardian of peace and good order.

As a body, we were only called into service on special occasions; but, as two or three of the boys were required to supply an occasional vacancy at the bellows, we were permitted to occupy the backless bench at the side of the organ; else, as a choir, we were disbanded as soon as the special purposes of the service were accomplished.

Congregational singing was nursed and promoted as a sacred duty, and nothing whatever was allowed to interfere, mar, or diminish it. Hence, the tune-book of the Church was closely adhered to; and the first line of any hymn found its melody in the ready evidences of a congregational swell of harmony.

Many of the verses of the Moravian Hymns being very long, some even of *ten* lines, and the peculiar metres being *very* peculiar, interludes between the lines, always befitting the subject, seemed a necessary relief to the voice, as well also as to keep up its strength to the pitch. This performance required tact, talent, skill, and practice, for a smooth and congenial connection of the context, but as the hymn was lined by the minister, in connection, one, two, or even three at a time, there were no freaks of fancy, as in these days, inflicted upon the congregation between the verses.

In a word, the Hymnology of the Church was as much a part of the *worship* as the prayers or preaching, since it comprises both, and as the minister *always* suited his hymns to the subject of his intended discourse, the organist, by his ticket, was duly apprised of his duty, and opened and continued the service accordingly. And it is a praiseworthy record to say, that to this day there has been very little, if any, infraction of this "faithful continuance in well-doing."

Whilst on this subject, I cannot forego the opportunity of protesting against the light, trifling, and even vulgar perpetrations, in the musical department of many of our sister churches; their constituents not only permitting, but encouraging, aiding, and abetting, the tritely called Young America, to victimize the sanctuary to the worldly begettings of Belial; desecrating the noble instrument of prayer, praise, and supplication, to the lowest degree of a street hand-organ, and subverting this happy medium to the heart, to the influences of a vain show, of a sickly, if not a depraved appetite, of an experimenting and irreligious candidate for worldly fame and popularity, altogether inconsistent with the place and the trust committed to him.

"Jesus Christ to be worshipped in spirit and in truth," whose religion never grows old, who requires the same now, as He did at the date of his personal precept and example, what say ye, brethren, is this to be *perfected* by the spirit of the age? He began in the Spirit, and so taught; are we to improve upon his *purity* by ending in the flesh? God forbid! let us return to our first Christian principles, lest He fulfil his threat, and remove our "candlestick out of his place." (Revelations 2 : 5.)

There is decidedly too much importance attached to the subsidiary end of the Church, in these days; too much encomium, or depreciation of the secondary consideration in the worship; all which is begotten by a thirst for amusement, or a sensual appetite for comparative popularity.

The minister may preach his throat sore, the *orchestra* takes the lead, and the compliments *to*, or the denunciation of the organist, or his choir, leave the wayworn prelate untold and unheralded, but not unswept, by the unhallowed breeze of all their thoughts of him or his holy doings. Popular melodies, hatched from operatic fancies, dragged into the Church, are but meagre apologies for plucking Satan of his so-called superior musical taste, and cannot fraternize nor sympathize with those emotions, which the heart should encourage in God's Holy Temple, to come out from the world, and be separate. If the Devil has the best tunes, let him keep them. "What has light to do with darkness, or Christ, with Belial?"

It may be one way to induce people to go to church, but a *dangerous far about* to a glorious eternity.

Sentences, motets, arias, and the like, are of modern date, and it is much to be feared are mere subterfuges for the deficiencies of a non-inventive genius. They are seldom, if ever, devotional, are no part of the service, and whether done well or ill, are a means of distraction of the sentiments due to or by a Christian assemblage. The invocation, however it may be harmonized and offered, amounts to nothing more than a vain exhibition of fancy, taste, skill, intonation, and all the concomitants of a worldly catering for popularity.

Neither were voluntaries or extemporizing in advance, or in the intermediate service of the Church, ever designed for exhibition of freakful fancy, nor as sparkling fountains of popular attraction, much less as competitors for the holy influences of the Divine order of the sanctuary. On the contrary, the opening voluntary was intended, and ever should be, a respectful development of a mind properly impressed with the sacred duties before the organist; edification is due at his hands, and intelligence from his mind.

"The Lord is in his holy temple;" the congregation is there to worship Him. His blessing has been silently invoked, and the emotions of the heart are awaiting the Spirit's increase; the breath of rhythmic harmony should therefore flow, a hallowed influence, to aid the ingathering from the sacred desk.

The intermediate voluntary should be a consistent acknowledgment of the past, an exordium to a faithful continuance in well-doing, as well, also, as a premonitory symptom of good things to come. Alas! how are we fallen! Alas! alas!

It is a lamentable fact, that after service in many churches, the interchange of sentiment is mostly on the subject of the music.

"Did you ever hear such miserable singing?" says one.

"Miss Smith was flat in her alto."

"Miss Brown—shocking! a regular screech! and such a tenor! why the man can't sing at all! and the bass, too, a bawl! why, we have better street-music! Well, if they don't have better music, I, for one, won't come to church!"

"But that sketch of 'Norma' was done well! and 'Sonnambula,' in the voluntary, just before the hymn, was splendid! but the hymn-tune—pshaw! what a bore!"

"Ha! you should go to St. ——'s; there they have it! 'Zampa,' 'Jeun Henri,' 'The Barber of Seville,' 'Last Rose of Summer!' Oh my, it is equal to a concert!"

Such, or the like, is too often the compliments to the minister, and the effect upon the members, or very many of them, of the dispersing throng. And who is to blame? In answer, we ask, Who has charge of this sacred duty? The rector, in conjunction with such of his vestry as are skilled in music. It is, of course, not to be presumed that every minister, in every place, is a musician; nor can we concede that all who *profess* to know something of this divine art, are competent to direct the choir; but they certainly ought to know the difference between the use and the abuse of the organ; they certainly can tell, if not by their senses by their sight, that "holiness belongeth to thine house, O Lord, forever," and that worldly fantasies cannot be so blended with that holiness, as to be mistaken for a motive to the petition to the Deity to "cleanse the thoughts of our hearts, by the inspiration of his holy Spirit."

Surely, if the shepherd of his flock should be wanting in judgment, in a matter so important, there must be some of his ingathering who could aid him in a consistent keeping of the church service.

But alas! the fatal thirst for popularity is too freely quenched at the wrong end of the church, and the "charms of the opera" imbibed, to the prejudice of the offerings from the sacred altar.

A volume might be written on the subject of musical liberties and improprieties in the Church, but my immediate purpose would be infringed by an elaboration of the evil; and, after my testimony against it, it behooves me to proceed to the more immediate purpose of my history, apologizing first for the digression.

This tabernacle of the Lord was in being from 1742 to 1819, a period of seventy-seven years.

Its influence, associations, and growth, have been fully, and I believe faithfully set forth.

The impressions of youth are not easily effaced, and a contemporaneous continuance with the things that were, grow a history in the recipient of current facts.

I have, therefore, no hesitation whatever in offering the preceding details, as a correct issue of memory, aided by data as authentic and reliable.

There were, however, officials important to the completion of this part of my history, which from the Records I now proceed to present.

CHAPTER XXVI.

Continuance of the Church History—Succession of Officers resumed and continued.

As there do not appear to have been any regular minutes from 1742 to 1785, it is probable that the supervision of this branch of the Church was confined to the ecclesiastical court at Bethlehem, whence came supplies, temporal and spiritual, as necessity required, whilst the brethren here accounted to that, as the head of the mission, for all their acts, domestic or ecclesiological, by protocol or diary.

The gathering in this period was small, and being confined to more immediate missionary purposes, record was lost sight of in the current of their missionary zeal, whilst their accountability passed to the source of their authority by occasional correspondence.

Pecuniary matters were of secondary consideration; they required but little, and having "godliness with contentment," "great gain" was their daily feast.

Time, however, began to show the fruits of their labor, and a closer or more local organization of the body was necessary; and hence it was deemed expedient, as it was quite practicable, for the elder brethren to put this youth of their "household of faith," now more mature, upon a more self-supporting platform.

Offices were then first created, and officers appointed to the respective secular duties of the Church.

Bishop de Watteville, therefore, as heretofore stated, came to Philadelphia for that purpose, and appointed the first Committee, viz.:

Bernhardt Adam Grube, and Jacob Fries,		Presiding Ministers.
Adam Goose, George Schlosser, John Peter, John Cornman,	George Senneff, Conrad Gerhardt, Godfrey Haga, Thomas Bartow,	A Standing Committee, or Vestry of the Church.

Of this body, Thomas Bartow was appointed Secretary by the Committee.

THE SUCCESSION OF THE MINISTRY.

The Brethren Grube and Fries seem to have been the central point of the organization for the time being, seeing that in the same year, 1785, Brother John Meder is the President of the Committee, and the others not named.

Brother John Meder served from October, 1785, to 1799, when he was called to serve the congregation in New York, and Brother John Frederick Frueauff filled the vacancy from 1799 to 1803; when, being called to the inspectorship of Nazareth Hall, Brother Joseph Zaeslein took his place here, and served from 1803 to 1812.

As a minister could not remain pastor of a congregation without a wife, and Sister Zaeslein having departed in this year, Brother Zaeslein was necessarily recalled, and, for the time being, located at Bethlehem.

Brother John C. Beckler was appointed his successor, remaining, however, only one year, 1812, 1813, when he was appointed to the station at Staten Island.

Brother John Meder resumed this station, *ad interim*, until a more regular appointment could be made; and sojourned here officially from 1813 to 1814, when he retired to Nazareth.

Brother John G. Miller, being called from his station at Muskingum, now became the incumbent, and served from 1814 to 1817, when, being called to Litiz, Pa.,

Brother William Henry Van Vleck assumed the pastorate by the regular course of appointment, and continued his services from 1817 to 1822; being then called to the inspectorship of Nazareth Hall.

Although the last named in this succession overruns the existence of the edifice, we cannot divide his time, but note his service to its terminus in Philadelphia.

Confining my history, therefore, to its immediate sphere, the clerical catalogue must give place here to the contemporaries of that day, and hence follows the succession of the subordinate officers.

The original Standing Committee continued from 1785 to 1794; diminished, however, by "death's doings," so that in March, 1794, an election to fill vacancies, declared the following result:

Brethren, Isaac Smallwood,
Jacob Ritter, Sen., and
Jacob Frank,
in place of deceased Brethren, Senneff,
Peter and Bartow.

In 1803, a general election became necessary from the same cause, and the Brethren

Conrad Gerhardt,
Godfrey Haga,
Jacob Frank,
Jacob Ritter, Sen.,
John Jordan, and
John Boller,

constituted the ruling authority of the Church.

1809, Brother Benjamin Lyndall was chosen in place of Brother John Boller, deceased.

1817, Brother Jacob Ritter, Jr., in place of Brother Conrad Gerhardt, deceased in 1814.

1818, Brother Thomas C. Lueders, in place of Brother B. Lyndall, deceased.

Thus far the Committee.

The Secretary was originally a member of their body, and was entitled of course to a vote, but subsequently was chosen from the congregation by the Committee, but ineligible to vote; in due time, however, they were admitted, or elected into the body. Frederick Boller was the first thus chosen.

1785 to 1792. Thomas Bartow.

1792 to 1794. Rev. John Meder, p. t., volunteer.

1794 to 1802. Frederick Boller, appointed.

1802 to 1809. John Boller, in place of his brother, Frederick Boller, deceased.

1809 to 1818. Jacob Ritter, Jr., place of John Boller, deceased.

1818 to 1825. John Wise Peters, in place of J. Ritter, Jr., elected to the Committee.

STEWARDS.

Thomas Bartow was the first steward and general accountant, and served from 1785 to 1792.

Brother Conrad Gerhardt succeeded him, and served from 1792 to 1814, when his son, William Gerhardt, held the office *ad interim*, 1814 to 1815, when Brother John Jordan, being duly appointed, held the office from 1815 to 1836, a period of twenty-one years.

TREASURERS.

1785 to 1814. Brother Conrad Gerhardt.
1814 to 1815. Brother Wm. Gerhardt, p. t.
1815 to 1834. J. Ritter, Jr.

COLLECTORS OF SUSTENTATION FUND.

1785. Brother George Schlosser.
1785 to 1788. Brother George Senneff.
1788 to 1793. Brother Godfrey Haga.
1793 to 1823. Brother Jacob Ritter, Sen., thirty years.

ALMONERS.

1785. Brother Conrad Gerhardt.
1788. Brother George Schlosser.
1788 to 1814. Brother Conrad Gerhardt.
1815 to 1836. Brother Wm. Gerhardt.

ORGANISTS.

George Peter and John Peter, were the organists of 1785, and Frederick Boller, John Boller, and Jacob Boller followed in succession.

The two former died in the service, and the latter resigned the charge into the hands of the writer, and Abraham Ritter, served from 1811 to 1843.

There being no salaried officers in the church, the organist also was a *voluntary de facto*, made so by common consent of the congregation, but in after-times, appointed by the Committee of the Church; but, from first to last, all the offices were more of trust and confidence than of profit.

CHAPEL SERVANTS.

1785 to 1787. Brother John Merck.
1787 to 1819. Brother Jacob Frank.
1787 to 1819. Brother Jacob Ritter, Sr.
1801 to 1804. Brother Zachariah Poulson.

SUPERINTENDENTS OF THE BURIAL-GROUND.

1786. Brother Jacob Ettwein had charge of the ground, under the title of Grave-digger. Several successions occurred from other outside officials, till 1812, when Brother Benjamin Lyndall, being duly appointed, served till 1818; and from 1818 to 1836, Brother J. Ritter, Jr., was the incumbent.

THE INVITERS.

These functionaries were by no means supernumeraries, but as important in their sphere as the *maître de chappelle* of a cathedral, in the catalogue of officers; and, therefore, justly and respectfully belong an historical tribute to Brother John Merck, who served from 1786 to 1794; and Henry Cress and George Gasner, of the Lutheran Church, as well as Peter Fenner, of the German Reformed Church, the survivor of his predecessors, and, doubtless, a very unwilling witness to the total annihilation of the office by the march of improvement.

The two last were within my own time. The former of these, Mr. Gasner, was a dapper little gentleman, active and intelligent, and always at home in good manners. The latter, less endowed by education, but proud of his calling, was equally at home in suavity and courteous civility.

Thus was constituted and thus stood the original Moravian Church in Philadelphia, and thus we hand it over to the antiquary, or the lover of ancient landmarks, to perpetuate its memory, and call it from the dying tones of its requiem of 1819.

But the furtherance of its purposes did not depart with the shades of the edifice. The foundation still remained, and Jesus Christ being its corner-stone, the Spirit waxed warm, and outgrew the confines of infancy, and an increase of border became absolutely necessary.

John Adam Goose, a German, born May 13th, 1712, immigrated to this country in 1740, and was probably an original member of the Society. Departed this life, November 28th, 1804; aged 92 years, 6 months, 9 days.

George Senneff departed September 11th, 1788, aged 57 years.

George Schlosser, a German merchant, departed February 25th, 1802; aged 87 years.

Conrad Gerhardt, born in Heidelberg Township, Pa., November 22d, 1740. Departed February 24th, 1815, in his 75th year.

John Benedict Peter, biscuit baker, departed October 10th, 1793, in his 64th year. He was a German.

John Everhard Cornman, a German, departed June 22d, 1794, in his 69th year.

Thomas Bartow, born in Perth Amboy, New Jersey. Departed January 26th, 1793; aged 56 years.

Godfrey Haga, a German, departed 1825.

Isaac Smallwood, born in Jersey; departed Jan. 7th, 1811, in his 56th year.

Jacob Ritter, Sr., born in Philadelphia, Nov. 18th, 1754; departed Nov. 3d, 1834, 80 years of age—less 15 days.

John Boller, a German; departed June 14th, 1808, in his 34th year.

John Jordan, Sr., born in Jersey; a grocer; departed Feb. 17th, 1845, in his 75th year.

Benjamin Lyndall, born near Philadelphia; departed July 28th, 1818, in his 56th year.

Jacob Ritter, Jr., born in Philadelphia; departed June 27th, 1840, in his 57th year.

John Frederick Boller, a German, and brother to John Boller; departed Nov. 24th, 1802, in his 35th year.

John W. Peter, born in Philadelphia; departed July 21st, 1830, in his 42d year.

John Peter, born in Philadelphia; departed Oct. 19th, 1793, in his 37th year.

George Peter, born in Philadelphia; departed May 11th, 1811, in his 48th year.

For Z. Poulson, see biographical sketch.

John Henry Merck, a Dane, born Sept. 6th, 1718; departed Aug. 28th, 1794, aged 77 years—less 9 days.

Abram Jacob Frank, born in Philadelphia, Oct. 11, 1743; departed Nov. 26th, 1819, aged 76 years, 1 month, and 15 days.

Jacob Boller, died Sept. 16th, 1851, aged 60 years.

CHAPTER XXVII.

The Destruction of the Old, and Erection of a New Building.

The increase of population, the din of business, and the popularity of Race Street and Moravian Alley as a thoroughfare, already in 1800 induced the suggestion of protecting their Sabbath quiet, by stretching chains across Race Street, and also Moravian Alley,—a practice of other churches of that day, and continued till 1820; when political feuds wrangled with Church authority, and party spirit, jealous of ecclesiastical privileges, petitioned and strove with the Legislature of Pennsylvania to abrogate the law of this indulgence.

In 1806, therefore, a removal was agitated, the locality being considered obscure to a spreading population, noisy as a thoroughfare, and the edifice inconvenient to a rising generation; but lack of funds, besides the difficulty of fixing upon any other location, left the matter for future consideration.

In 1816 and 1817 again the subject was more earnestly considered, and an eye to the burial-ground set with some determination, but the want of unanimity on this fixture disjointed the proceeding, and action was suspended.

In 1819, however, necessity urged its claims. The natural increase of the congregation was enhanced by the

Hayes & Zell, Publ. Phil^a

Lith. by Herline & Hensel, Phil^a

THE MORAVIAN CHURCH OF 1820.

S.E. Corner of Moravian Alley (Now Race St.) & Race St.

popularity of its pastor, the Rev. W. H. Van Vleck, induced as well by his unadorned oratory and manner, as the Spirit-endowed matter. Untiring in zeal, and winning in its application, he reached the heart kindly, and smote the unrighteous friendly, and warmed the atmosphere of his presence with the sincerity and truth of his effusions, and the unmistakable halo of humility.

The practical and pious issues of this "man of God," as once hailed by our venerable Bishop Hueffel, are too well known and fresh in the memory of many of his contemporaries, to need an apology for this limited but truthful tribute to his memory.

There was, however, another impetus to the maturity of the deliberations.

Until 1817, the services had been performed alternately in German and English, respectively, on every other Sunday; in this year, however, the rising generation, untaught in German, joined the mass in vetoing the future use of the language in the services of the Church, and a vote having been taken on the subject, gave the English party a decided majority, there being then very few surviving Germans in the church.

This, with the satisfactory qualification of the rector, compelled the Committee to unbend their limits, increase their borders, and embrace the offerings for a more extensive gathering.

The burial-ground being still a favorite idea with many of the congregation as an eligible site, the subject was thoroughly canvassed; but was lost in the majority of objections, as well local as general and social.

Absence of funds to buy a lot elsewhere, as well as a diversity of opinion as to a central point, left but the alternative to dispossess the original of its venerable charge, and replace it with a more modern, a more convenient, and a more extensive structure.

In the month of February, therefore, A. D. 1819, the full maturity of the subject resulted in an engagement with Joseph Worrel, a member of the Society, to erect a church edifice on the old site, leaving the orginal parsonage still to dignify the place of its birth.

Wherefore, the structure was placed twelve feet from the southern line of the parsonage, extending east and west, across the rear of the two Race Street lots, forty-four feet, and north and south fifty-three feet, leaving a passage on the west of about five feet, and one on the east of eleven feet, together with a passage on the south of five feet, for the comforts and conveniences of light and air, and a passage from Race Street to the front of the church of twenty feet in width, by forty-seven feet, being the distance from the line of Race Street.

The front entrance of the church was guarded by a small vestibule, of about five feet in depth and ten in breadth, having a door at each side opening to the stairway of the galleries, as well as to the area below; but for the more convenient egress of the congregation, a large folding door formed the centre of the partition.

The elevation of the building was two feet six inches, leaving only space below for a current of air.

A cellar was objected to, lest at some future period it might be let for the storage of malt or spirituous liquors.

The height of the building was twenty-nine feet to the eaves, and thirty-six feet to the apex.

The interior arrangement was plain and unadorned.

The pulpit was a meagre apology for a sightly rostrum,

as are a majority of that important appurtenance of the present day, and which require but one more idea to convert into oyster-boxes! They are at best miserable and mean substitutes for the old-style real pulpits; and there was style in the beautiful panelled breastwork of polished mahogany, with easy curve at either side, rising with dignity to the platform, or for the characteristic pedestal, with neatly covered table and chair beneath, difficult to pervert by thought, or convert by act, to any use than the mount to elevate a Gospel herald.

The nook, a very small room—the vacuum of the box before us—was an antechamber to the church area, and was about eight by twelve in dimensions, having a quick stairway to the platform above, and a door of ingress and egress at each side. It was contrived a double debt to pay, being as well a conservative, for the preparation of love-feasts, as the private receptacle of the minister before and after service.

For the rest, the furniture was simplified into plain benches, cushioned only as a desideratum to age or infirmity.

The side galleries were nine feet deep, but the organ gallery on the north end was twelve feet deep; in which was placed, in 1825, an organ built by E .N. Scherr, of the following disposition.

Pedal, c.c. 1 double diapason, 16 feet.
1 open, 8 feet, or octave.

Great Organ. Bordun, 16 feet (very heavy).
Stopped Diapason, 8 feet.
Open Diapason, 8 feet.
Hollow Flute, 8 feet.
Principal, 8 feet.
Trumpet, 8 feet.

Swell. Stopped Diapason.
Flute.
Dulciana.
Principal.

This organ had no reeds beyond the trumpet, was of very heavy tone, and, as will be seen, had nothing to elasticize it.

Its cost was $1200, besides the organ previously in use, which cost the church $400.

The corner-stone of the building was laid on the 12th of May, 1819; and the work prosecuted under the supervision of the following members, as a Building Committee, to wit:

Daniel Man, Jacob Boller,
Francis Kampman, William Gerhard, and
George Ritter,

and was consecrated on the 12th of December, of the same year.

Bishop Hueffel, our presiding Bishop, unable to be present, sent the proper credentials to Brother Van Vleck, who presided at the ceremonies, and was aided by the Rev. Mr. Cruze, of the English Lutheran Church, and Dr. Helmuth, of the German Lutheran Church.

William H. Van Vleck
p. t. Pastor of the United Brethren's
Church at Philadelphia.

CHAPTER XXVIII

The Interregnum—Demolition of the Original Parsonage.

During the process of rebuilding, the public worship was held in the old Academy, in Fourth below Arch Streets; whilst the private meetings, Holy Communion, pedelavium, baptisms, love-feasts, &c., were administered in the attic of the old parsonage. This apartment, denuded of its partitions, was rendered of sufficient capacity to accommodate all of the closer members of the church, the organ, the benches, and the chair and table of the hall, being removed there, and conveniently arranged for their intended purposes.

The organ, being placed at the southeast corner of the room, having a window at its side, was made available as the accompaniment to the sacred song below, during the performance of the ceremony of laying the corner-stone of the new church edifice; the effect of which was both interesting and very acceptable. On the centre of the eastern wall of this room, stood the minister's table and chair, elevated about six inches; at each side were wall benches, and in front of the table, the general congregational accommodations; the brethren to the left of the minister, and the sisters on his right.

THE DEMOLITION OF THE OLD PARSONAGE.

As time and tide wait for no man, so American enterprise spares nothing. We compass sea and land in search of antiquities, but destroy our own the very moment that they ripen to that dignity.

This venerable pile was an original in Philadelphia, dignified, not only by time, but by its services, fraught with characteristic and interesting associations, tributary as well to the life of imagination as to its more happy source.

"Young America," yet unborn, and even unthought, was anticipated by an inkling for novelty, whilst the "march of improvement" in embryo, was courting discipline and furtherance, and, not unlike the youth of our day, pressing its claims, its fancy, and its wisdom, spurned the taste, the judgment, and the wisdom of our fathers; and the very shadows of antiquity must be absorbed in the glory of their imagination. But so it was; and even worse now. Still, we cannot but marvel at our old-time predecessors, for yielding the precious mementos of their own times, to the very questionable apologies for their affections.

Whatever may have been the inducement for such old-time folks to disrupt the precious relic of their *own* times, beyond the impetus of modern fancy, is hard to say; certain it is, this last relic of Zinzendorff and his times, in Philadelphia, this convenient, capacious, comfortable, respectable legacy of their fathers, must merge into a residuum of a mere apology for a substitute.

Alas! alas! such is the spirit of the age in America; but doubtful elsewhere in the world!

This ancient pile, sacred to the memory of every contemporaneous Moravian in Philadelphia, the relic of its adjunct the original church—was, for a season, the bosom of its more immediate sacerdotal rites.

It was the mansion of the "rites of hospitality—the home of the missionary"—the *alma mater* of Christian benevolence! Religion and piety dwelt there; mercy and truth met there; and there, too, righteousness and peace often kissed each other.

Spangenberg, Nitchman, Boehler, and the host of early pioneers in the wilderness of Sin, met, conferred, and dispensed their spiritual might to destroy the schemes and devices of Satan.

De Watteville, Loskiel, Reichel, and Hueffel, of later times, came here to light up the path of the elders, to rule well their household of faith, and to assist them in prayer for the peace and prosperity of their Zion!

Dissensions and doubtful disputations were arrested here, and the atmosphere of its portals was redolent of harmony, seeing that it was a court of appeal for the settlement of error or misunderstanding of or amongst the members of the flock.

The doctrine of mutual forbearance here had sway, "if any man had a quarrel against any;" and mutual forgiveness was a *sine qua non* to admission to the next succeeding communion or love-feast.

The goodly pastor was the arbiter, and a godly issue was the general reward of his labor of love.

In all this I do not mean to idolize the temple nor its adjunct, the parsonage, nor yet would I canonize Moravians or Moravianisms at any period of their existence; but with such associations, justice to their manes cannot reject a tribute to the odor that even yet enriches our atmosphere of the incense of their faith, principles, and practices, as it arose from the altar of their hearts.

CHAPTER XXIX.

The Renewal, and Change of Location.

SOLOMON has said that time and chance "happeneth to all men," and this, for several years past, had been a hoped for desideratum in this congregation.

The building of 1819 was not only very inconvenient, but was thrown into obscurity by the populous expanse of the city, so that the West knew little of the East, whilst the North and the South began to fringe the rural domains of the city's pride.

The escutcheons of the tabernacle had lost their lustre, whilst the ruthless hand of Time wrestled with the treasury, and touched the spirit of the age.

Improvements and repairs had drawn smartly upon taste and ambition, until genius and invention were beggared by the want of material for their exercise.

The congregation had increased, and the rising generation claimed the privilege of enjoying some of the fascinations of their *own* times.

The question, therefore, of a new church, and a more eligible site, was long and elaborately agitated, before the idea settled to a more serious and decided consideration.

In the spring of 1853, reflection matured, and the congregation, in due form, ordered the sale of the old premises, together with all the appurtenances, and further ordained, that a new church edifice should be built upon a new site.

A committee was appointed to look out for a lot, and report.

A lot on Green Street, north side, below Eleventh, now occupied as a Methodist Church, was reported, but declined from motives of economy, prudence, and expediency; and the Burial-ground, being a favorite idea for eligibility, convenience, and practicability, it was adopted as the site for the new church.

One year, however, elapsed before anything like an offer could be obtained for a private sale of the old premises; and the congregation growing restive under the delay, a public sale was ordered.

On the evening of the 7th of March, 1854, the property was put up for public sale by Moses Thomas & Son, at the Exchange, and there purchased, by Conrad Grove, for the small sum of $16,000, who sold it the next day, or within a week, to Robert Newlin, brewer, at a smart advance.

The lot is sixty by one hundred and twenty feet, containing the church building on the rear, and two three-story brick dwellings on Race Street.

Considerable delay followed these preliminaries, so that preparations for a commencement of the enterprise were protracted till the spring of 1855; when, according to a plan and architectural drawing, made and presented to the Building Committee by Mr. J. A. C. Trautwine, a member of the church, a contract was made with Mr. John McClure, a respectable and reliable builder, to carry out the project.

The Burial-ground being twenty-five feet short of the corner of Franklin and Wood, and that spot being already occupied by a three-story brick dwelling, a purchase was absolutely necessary to reach and establish the desired boundary of the edifice.

Peter Marseiles, awake to our requirements and alive to his own, demanded the full sum of $7500 for the premises, which must be paid, and that in a given time, or lose the site.

This sum was, therefore, paid, and the house doomed to destruction in the contract with Mr. McClure, which stipulated for this building, and $14,700.

Preliminaries, therefore, being at an end, the corner-stone was laid on the 30th day of April, 1855, and the edifice consecrated on the 26th of January, 1856.

The Building Committee consisted of Abraham Ritter, Francis Jordan, Jacob E. Hagert, and Charles L. Bute.

The corner-stone was laid by the Right Rev. Peter Wolle, a Bishop of the Church, aided by the *pastor loci*, the Rev. Edmund A. de Schweinitz, the Brethren Bahnsen, Shultz, and others of the Moravian Church, besides of our sister churches, the venerable Dr. Mayer of the English Lutheran Church; the Rev. J. Berg and Bamberger of the German Reformed Churches.

CHAPTER XXX.

Change of Location—Description of the New Edifice—Organ.

The building occupies fifty-five by eighty feet of the southwest corner of Wood and Franklin Streets, a passage of about six feet being left on the south side, convenient to the rear door of the church from Franklin Street.

The lower or basement floor is conveniently arranged with vestibule, of twelve feet in depth, opening into a lecture and Sunday-school room, of about fifty-three feet square, and eleven feet in height; in the rear of which is the minister's room, on the north side, and on the south, an apartment for "love-feast" arrangements, and other appurtenant conveniences to the services of the church; the ascent to the pulpit being also from the minister's room.

The principal audience chamber is attained by an open Newell stairway on each side of the vestibule, of very easy ascent, and sufficient capacity for their purpose.

An upper vestibule passes the congregation, as they enter by a door at the head of each stairway, into this principal accommodation for the public worship, whose area is covered with eighty pews, without doors, of sufficient dimensions to seat five hundred persons comfortably. The aisles open at each of the entrances, and consequently give a middle block and wall pews, but no centre aisle.

The pulpit is a neat elevation, of about three feet, protected at either side by a fancy screen of "gig-saw work," and immediately behind by a close panelled screen, supported at each end by heavy bosses of gothic fancy, rising some eight or ten feet from the stairway, opening upon the pulpit's platform.

The table and chair in front of the pulpit, for communion, baptismal, and reception services, surmount a platform of six inches in height, but are not enclosed by screen or railing of any sort.

The organ gallery in front, at the east end of the chamber, has an elevation of nine feet, and in architectural design corresponds in fashion with the protective screen of the pulpit's platform.

These two ends are painted and grained in imitation of walnut, except the front panel on the pulpit, which relieves the monotony, by the very appropriate insignia of a "gloria," richly gilt.

The ends of the pews are painted and grained in imitation of oak, the top rail and arms, however, represent walnut.

The pews are lined, stuffed, cushioned, and carpeted, whilst the aisles, the pulpit platform, its risers at each side, and the elevation below, are neatly clad in Brussels and ingrain, of taste and quality much to the credit of their patrons.

The gallery supports an organ of dignity, character, and corresponding architecture, designed under the direction of your author, and executed by Mr. Edmund Durang as architect, and Mr. J. C. B. Standbridge, whose skill, taste, and judgment is very creditably exemplified in its organic details.

Its outer dimensions are eighteen feet front, eight feet in depth, and twenty-nine feet to the top of the centre tower.

Its disposition is as follows:

Two sets of keys and pedals.

Great organ, compass, C, C, to F,	54 keys.	
1. Open Diapason, metal,	54 pipes.	
2. Stopped do. wood,	54 "	
3. Principal, 4 feet, metal,	54 "	
4. Melodeon, 4 feet, metal,	42 "	
5. Twelfth,	54 "	
6. Fifteenth,	54 "	
7. Seventeenth,	54 "	
8. Nineteenth and Twenty-second, 2 rank sesquialtera,	108 "	
9. Clarionet to tenor D,	40 "	
10. Slide for a trumpet.		
	——	514.
Swell with choir bass.		
11. Violin to 4 féet C, metal,	42 pipes,	
12. Stopped Diapason, wood,	54 "	
13. Principal, metal,	54 "	
14. Chimney-flute, metal,	42 "	
15. Fifteenth, metal,	42 "	
16. Two rank Cornet, metal,	84 "	
17. Trumpet, metal,	42 "	
	——	360.
Pedal-compass, C, C, C, to G,	20 keys.	
18. Double open Diapason, wood, 16 feet C, to 8 feet C,	13 "	
19. Dulciana, wood,	13 "	

20. Couples, great organ and swell.
Registers. 21. Couples, pedal and great organ.

Pipes, 900.

The cost of this instrument was $2000, and it is but justice to Mr. Standbridge to acknowledge his skill and scientific acumen in this exuberance of his genius.

The silken tones of the stopped Diapason, the proclivity of his imitations to the orchestral reed, and the silvery rays from the mystic violin, together with the rich brilliancy of the lighter elasticity of the combination, needs no praise beyond their own utterance; yet "honor to whom honor is due."

The front pipes are beautifully gilt, and the case painted and grained* to correspond with the pulpit and gallery front.

The architectural design of the church edifice is of the Norman order, but modernized to suit the present age. Its location is certainly very beautiful, being on the summit of Franklin Street, open to Vine Street, and diagonally to the Square on the south—the Burial-ground lying between, affording light, air, and accessibility, as far as we can see, for all time.

The disparity between the early and the latter building being an evident departure from the pristine order, would seem to require reconciliation. Time and circumstance, however, will have sway, and locomotion neither lags nor limps.

It must be remembered that the Zinzendorffian edifice, though unostentatious, was large and imposing for its day.

His society consisted of thirty-four members, and yet

* By Wooldridge.

his building would accommodate from one hundred to one hundred and fifty persons.

The second building was but a slight improvement in form and feature, sufficiently attractive for its generation, but enlarged to meet the exigencies of its day.

The rise and progress of the congregation having kept full pace with the times, and the developments of the spirit of the age being epidemic in their nature, a propitiatory sacrifice to the outer form must necessarily be made, to gather up and protect the "inner man;" and hence, to meet the views of the ingathering, a suitable invitation to their presence was as laudable as it was necessary and expedient; but, notwithstanding, we may say, in this sense, with the Apostle, "Though our outer man has perished, our inner man remains."

Although the Church does not approve of any extravagance of outlay for fancy or fashion for its buildings, still a suitable medium to the altar of God cannot be deprecated; and if the offering is not made by us, it is or will be by others, and our congregation necessarily scatters from our fold.

Many years ago, when a splendid building was being put up for the Rev. G. T. Bedell, who had been preaching in a byway, and who was "mighty in word and deed," and yet a very plain, unassuming, practical Christian brother, I asked him how he could reconcile such an edifice with his plain views of humility? His reply was, "I must preach where people will come to hear me; to me it matters not where." We therefore offer necessity for expediency, and church patriotism as an apology for the disparity.

CHAPTER XXXI.

The Succession—The Ministry—Incorporation—Continued.

THE pastorate of Brother W. H. Van Vleck was filled at his recall, in 1822, by the Rev. Samuel Renike, who served one year, and was succeeded by the Rev. John G. Herman, who served until 1826, when he being called to Lancaster, Brother Peter Wolle assumed the charge until 1836; thence to 1842, Brother David Bigler, a missionary from Antigua; thence by Brother Henry A. Schults, Sept. 1, 1842, to June, 1844, and *ad interim*, Brother Wm. H. Benade, until November of the same year.

The regular official appointment of Brother Emanuel Rondthaler supplied the church from November, 1844, until his demise, on the 30th of November, 1848, when another *ad interim* appointment of Brother Edward Reichel linked the succession from December, 1848, to April, 1849, when it was regularly continued under charge of Brother Edward Rondthaler, a brother of the deceased Emanuel, until August, 1853.

Brother Edmund A. De Schweinitz, the present pastor, accepted the call and appointment to the pastorate in August, 1853, vacated by an appointment elsewhere of his predecessor.

THE STANDING COMMITTEE.

Of this body, vacancies had been and were yet filled as they occurred, by death or otherwise.

The last of this custom under the old *régime* was as before stated.

1818. Thomas C. Lueders, in place of Benjamin Lyndall, deceased, and thus continued.

1821. Adam Neiss, in place of Brother Jacob Frank, deceased.

1822. Joseph Lyndall, in place of Adam Neiss, expelled.

1825. John W. Peter and George Esler, in place of Godfrey Haga, and Joseph Lyndall, deceased.

1830. Abraham Klewel, in place of J. W. Peter, deceased.

1834. A general election produced the following result, for three years' service:

Brother John Jordan,	Thos. C. Lueders,
John Binns,	Charles L. Bute,
Valentine Hent,	Abraham Ritter.

1837. Brother Hent declined re-election, and the following brethren were duly elected:

John Jordan,	John Binns,
Thomas C. Lueders,	Charles L. Bute,
Charles Williams,	Abraham Ritter.

1840.	John Binns,	Abraham Ritter,
	Chas. L. Bute,	Valentine Hent,
	Wm. Boller,	Chas. Williams.
1843.	John Bimms,	Valentine Hent,
	Joseph Cake,	Abraham Ritter,
	Wm. Boller,	Thos. W. Jones.

1846.	George Esler,	Wm. Boller,
	John Binns,	Fredk. Wilhelm,
	A. B. Renshaw,	Alex. Leimer.

Brother W. Boller having deceased in the interim, Brother T.W. Jones was again called in to fill the vacancy.

1849.	A. B. Renshaw,	T. W. Jones,
	Philip A. Cregar,	Chas. Williams,
	Alex. Smith,	Fredk. Bourquin.
1852.	A. B. Renshaw,	T. W. Jones,
	P. A. Cregar,	Francis Jordan,
	F. Bourquin,	Abraham Ritter.
1855.	Francis Jordan,	Abraham Ritter,
	A. B. Renshaw,	P. A. Cregar,
	C. M. S. Leslie,	C. L. Bute.

But C. M. S. Leslie having declined service, and Brother Charles Williams being the next highest on the ticket, was constituted a member in his place.

THE INCORPORATION.

Up to the year 1847, the Moravian Church, in Philadelphia, knew no need of incorporation; it had nothing to lend, and no imperious necessity to borrow; it had no need to plead, and gave no cause to be impleaded.

She had never run into the jaws of the law; nor had the law ever known of its being.

As a missionary circle, it was respected and protected by friend or foe—if any it had of the latter.

Notwithstanding, the Standing Committee of 1847 deemed it wise to have the act, and they obtained it; having the future ruling body, heretofore called "Committee," denominated "Elders," so that from 1847 to 1855, and further, they are, and are to be called "Elders."

STEWARDS.

The stewardship was continued successively as follows:

Brother John Jordan was succeeded by

"	Thos. C. Lueders,	1836–1838.
"	Chas. L. Bute,	1838–1842.
"	Valentine Hent,	1842–1845.
"	Thos. W. Jones,	1845–1846.
"	Fredk. Wilhelm,	1846–1849.

SECRETARIES.

1825–1833. Henry J. Boller, in place of J. W. Peters.

1833–1836. John P. Binns, " Henry J. Boller, resigned.

1836–1840. Abraham Ritter, " John P. Binns, resigned.

1840–1847. Wm. Boller, " Abraham Ritter, resigned.

TREASURERS OF SUSTENTATION ACCOUNT.

Brother	John Binns,	1834–1846.
"	Fredk. Wilhelm,	1846–1849.
"	A. B. Renshaw,	1849–1852.
"	Francis Jordan,	1852 to date and onwards.

COLLECTORS OF SUSTENTATION FUND.

Brother Jacob Ritter, Sen., was succeeded by

"	Joseph Lyndall,	1823–1824.
"	Abrm. Ritter,	1824–1828.
"	John W. Peters,	1828–1830.

Brother	Thomas C. Lueders and Geo. Esler,	1830–1832.
"	V. Hent place of T. C. Lueders,	1834–1836.
"	J. P. Binns " G. Esler,	1834–1836.
"	Wm. Boller vice V. Hent,	1836–1839.
"	Geo. Ritter alone,	1839–1842.
"	Geo. Esler,	1842.

ALMONERS.

Abraham Ritter, vice Wm. Gerhard,	1836–1846.
F. Wilhelm,	1846–1849.
A. B. Renshaw,	1849–1852.
Abrm. Ritter,	1852 to date.

ORGANISTS.

This office was filled alternately, from 1844 to 1856, by the brethren:

Jacob Boller, Andrew G. Kern, Jr.,
C. D. Senseman, Abrm. Ritter,
Fred'k Wilhelm and his very efficient daughter, Miss Mary Wilhelm; but finally, falls again, Feb. 1856, into the incumbency of Abraham Ritter.

CHAPEL SERVANTS.

Under the old system, including the services of Zachariah Poulson, this and all the other sub-offices were without fee or reward; but the new church of 1819 called for more attention, and the gratuitous "housemaid" having passed this for a less onerous ordeal, regular appointments became necessary, though, even then, at a mere compensatory stipend for outlay.

Adam Neiss served for one year, but being expelled in the same year, 1820,

Brother G. Ritter accepted the office, at $60 per annum, and served from 1820 to 1832.

Brother Samuel Cregar succeeded him, and served from 1832 to 1839.

Brother	Alexander Smith,	1839–1841.
"	Anthony Keyser,	1841–1844.
"	Samuel Cregar,	1844–1847.
"	Frederick Wilhelm,	1847–
"	Anthony Keyser,	to date.

SUPERINTENDENT OF THE BURIAL-GROUND.

Brother J. Ritter, Jr., was succeeded by
George Ritter, 1836–1849, and he by
Frederick Bourquin, 1849–1855, and by
George W. Ritter, 1855 to date.

Unimportant as this detail may seem to the common reader, it still belongs to the history of the Church, and serves to show, from first to last, its humble and unaspiring temperament, carrying out our Saviour's injunction, "He that is greatest among you, let him be as the younger, and he that is chief, as he that doth serve." Luke, chap. 22, verse 26; besides the tribute of perpetuity of the memory of some very excellent brethren of the Church.

The history of the Church, from its foundation in Philadelphia, is thus comprised; derived from authentic sources, collateral evidences, early and continuous associations, official duties, and very reliable tradition.

It is by no means offered as a vain show of temporal

prosperity; but as the happy issue of a "faithful continuance in well-doing." "Paul planted and Apollos watered, but God gave the increase," and to Him, the Triune Father, Son, and Holy Ghost, we will "render the calves of our lips," in the ascription of the Psalmist: "Not unto us, O Lord, not unto us, but unto thy name give glory, for thy mercy and for thy truth's sake." Amen. (Hosea 14 : 2; Psalm 115 : 1.)

BIOGRAPHICAL SKETCHES

OF SEVERAL OF THE

EARLY BISHOPS OF THE CHURCH.

CHAPTER XXXII.

THE EPISCOPACY.

NOTWITHSTANDING the proposed limits of my history, the mere name of an Episcopate would seem to fall short of evidence of her prelatical claims.

A general history of the Church was not my purpose, but the American, and more particularly the Philadelphia portion of the general *tome* of Moravianism, though but a mere paragraph of her extensive volume, can only be properly acknowledged by a proper and an authentic ecclesiastical representation.

To this end, I present the following sketches and portraits of some of their worthy subjects, as well as to light up the paths of our fathers to our own view, to confirm our acknowledgment of their authority, and to enjoy the happy association in our claims upon their right hand of fellowship, not in vanity nor vainglory, nor to cover our weakness with their strength, but if by any means we may "stand in the ways, and see, and ask for the old paths, where is the good way, and walk therein" (Jer. 6 : 16); and may the Lord grant us grace, to hearken to this sound of his trumpet.

BISHOP JOHN AMOS COMENIUS.

JOHN AMOS COMENIUS was born at Konma, in Moravia, on the 28th of March, 1592, and at a very early period of his life devoted himself to the ministry of the Gospel, in the Brethren's Church.

Banished in 1627 (with other Protestants), he fled to Poland, and settled at Lissa, where, at a synod, in 1632, he was consecrated a Bishop of the Bohemian and Moravian branch of the Brethren's Church, and thus became the connecting link of the episcopacy, from the ancient to the renewed Church of his adoption.

Reliable history sets him forth as a man of extensive erudition, an accomplished linguist, a practical self-sacrificing Christian, and a large contributor to the Christian Bibliothèque.

In 1649, he published a history of the Brethren's Church, with an appendix, dedicating the work, as his last will and testament, to the Church of England, asking her protection, preservation, and furtherance of the successors of the Brethren's Church, if she should survive her then low estate. Saying,

"Should it please God at a future period to educe good from our present affliction, and, according to his promise, make Christendom (after receiving wholesome correction), instrumental in propagating the Gospel among other nations, and do with us as he did with the Jews, cause our fall to be the riches of the world, and our diminishing

JOHN AMOS COMENIUS.

Episcopus.

the riches of the Gentiles, we, in that case, commend to you, the English Church, our beloved mother, the Brethren's Church, that you may take care of her, whatever it may please God to do with her, whether to restore her in her native land, or when deceased there, revive her elsewhere.

"Thus did God of old; for when he removed his ungrateful people from their country, and laid waste their city and temple, he did not suffer the basis of the altar to be destroyed, that after the return of his people from captivity, their successors might rebuild the temple on its former foundation," &c. &c. And closing thus:

"Into your hands, therefore, we commit this precious deposit, and thus, by your care, make provision for posterity."

The above work was written in Latin, and republished in English, in London, in 1661.

This venerable prelate and energetic patron of the Church, departed this life, on the 15th of October, 1672, aged eighty years; a volume in himself of faith and good works.

JOHN DE WATTEVILLE, EPISCOPUS.

"I DETERMINED to know nothing amongst you save Jesus Christ, and him crucified."

In this spirit came forth from the University of Jena, this disciple of theology, for the growth and increase of the ministry in the Brethren's Church, whose talents, developed through a liberal education and fervent zeal in the cause of Christianity, furthered him to the Episcopacy.

He was not of noble birth, but the son of the Rev. John Michael Langguth, a Lutheran minister, of Welsleben, in Thuringia, and born on the 18th of October, 1718.

As preceptor of a son of Count Zinzendorff, he enjoyed the approbation of the Father, and through a growing mutual interest and confidence became a convert, in 1737, to the principles and doctrines of Count Zinzendorff's adoption, and so early as 1739 took the general superintendence of the several institutions of the Church, during his absence from Herrnhuth and visit to the settlements in the West India Islands, besides the secretaryship of the Synods at Gotha and Marienborn, of 1740.

In 1744, he was appointed assistant to the Count in his ecclesiological duties, or chief official in the Church.

The Baron Frederick Von Watteville, his senior in the Church, propitious to his character, moral and religious, adopted him in this year, and endowed him with his titles.

JOHN DE WATTEVILLE,
Episcopus.

Clad, however, in the spirit of humility, he was in nowise inflated by this honor, and his ambition for title was acceptably merged in the familiar term of "Brother Johannes," which he preferred, and to which he answered through life, a custom prevalent in that circle of that day. Zinzendorff, also, was familiarly called "Brother Ludwig;" Spangenberg, "Brother Joseph."

In 1746, he became son-in-law to the Count by marriage with his eldest daughter, Henrietta Justina Benigna, and in 1747, was consecrated a Bishop of the Unitas Fratrii.

His duties were increased by obligatory visits to his churches and missionary stations in the very opposite directions of their various locations, and the Danish West Indies, Pennsylvania, England, Ireland, Holland, Greenland, by visits and revisits, made him a stranger to his proper home—Herrnhuth; until the death of Zinzendorff, in 1760, required his substitution there.

Available at all points, he was elected, in 1764, a member of the Directory, afterwards called the "Unity's Elder's Conference," the authority of the Church, which seat he held during the balance of his life.

In September, 1783, he was deputed to visit the congregations in North America, and set sail in that month, but when in sight of land, January, 1784, the ship, blown off by the charge of wintry blasts, was compelled to run for the West India Islands, and here, again,* the cliffs of the Island of Barbadoes arrested their escape from their recent perils, and wrecked them beyond alternative, except open boats, which, under God, saved him, his wife,

* On the night of February 16, 1784, a voyage of five months from the Texel to America.

and other brethren and sisters, together with the ship's crew, after a further toil and peril of seven hours.

With grateful considerations for the Governor of the Island, whose kindly care and furtherance of these servants of God justly entitles him to this memorabilia, I pass our venerable Bishop, and his consort, to Bethlehem, Pennsylvania, his place of destination; where, in June, 1784, he again "fed" the flock of God, "taking the oversight, not by constraint, but willingly" (1 Peter 5 : 2), and amongst the pleasing reminiscences of the Church in Philadelphia, its organization in 1785, the Apostolic salutation to "love one another," and his benediction, there can be none more interesting, more continuous, nor more animating, than a review of the ministration of "Brother Johannes," this venerable, plain, unvarnished prelate, breathing the virtues of Christianity from the Mount Sinai of the Ancient Church of our Philadelphia.

A three years' sojourn in America terminated his eventful and useful services from home. In June, 1787, he embarked for his final rest; and, after another year's services in the Church, at Herrnhuth, was called to his reward, on the 7th October, 1788, being 69 years of age, save 11 days.

The reputation of Bishop Von Watteville is that of an "intelligent, experienced, discreet, and faithful servant of Christ." A man whose fortitude never forsook him, and whose industry never tired.

Humility in him was the parent of affability, and merged the dignity of his Episcopate in the current and familiar associations with the flocks of his pastorate; and his prayer was ever and anon, "Not unto us, O Lord, not unto us, but unto thy name be all the glory."

Practical in precept and example, he won the confidence of his people, and reached their weaknesses by the chastened disciplining of his own.

But it is no part of my purpose to eulogize the man, or prejudice his memory, by an array of his virtues, but rather centre the memoir in the breathings of his own soul, and let the words of his own mouth, and the meditations of his own heart, sculpture his epitaph on the tablet of Time, in St. Paul's inscription, "By the grace of God, I am what I am." (1 Cor. 15 : 10.)

AUGUST GOTTLIEB SPANGENBERG, EPISCOPUS.

This eminent divine, patron, and early father in God, of the renewed Brethren's Church, was as world-wide known in his day, as his labors have since been blest to the various fields of his operations. He, also, was the son of a Lutheran minister, of Klettenburg, Prussia, where he was born, on the 15th of July, 1704. He studied theology at the University of Jena, of which he afterwards became a Professor, as well as that of Halle. Here he became acquainted with Count Zinzendorff; their kindred spirits blended, and unitedly strove for channels in which the softening influences of religion would flow to the rigid climes of such as were "sitting in darkness."

In 1733, he joined Zinzendorff at Herrnhuth, and soon became his adjunct in his views and plans for the spread of the Gospel.

From 1735 to 1744, Copenhagen, London, Georgia, and Pennsylvania, were beneficiaries of his labors of love.

In 1744, he was consecrated Bishop of the Brethren's Church;* and, as such, came to America, and took up his residence, on the 30th of November of that year, in Bethlehem.

Here, like St. Paul, he had the "care of all the churches," and gave himself to their supervision, whether afar off, or

* By Bishop Zinzendorff and Bishop F. de Watteville, Vicar-General of the three Tropics, in puncto ordinationis, first Bishop of the English Colonies.

Joseph, alias Augustus
Gottlieb Spangenberg

Episcopus.

near at hand. Wachovia, in N. C., Philadelphia, Lancaster, Bethlehem, Nazareth, and Litiz, in Pennsylvania, were all tenants of the shadow of his wing; and nursed, nurtured, and fructified by the influence of the divinity within; whilst his friendly hand and benign countenance at Indian councils in the South and West, won their confidence in the wisdom of his head, as well as in the truth of his heart, as it spent its holy burden at his lips.

His visits to these extreme stations were neither pondered nor deferred, for their threats of labor, sorrows, or difficulty. The fruit was at the extreme of the branches, and he sought to nurture it to ripeness, before it should fall.

A call to a spiritual charge in London deprived the American churches of his services in 1749; but, in 1751, he returned, and gladdened the hearts of his flocks, as for and during eleven years of further sympathy, he lit up their path in their council, their sanctuary, and their social intercourse.

In 1762, therefore, he took a final leave of America, passing through Philadelphia, leaving a lasting blessing upon his church, by his "savor of life unto life," which had so often and so richly bedewed the atmosphere of his spiritual operations.

Herrnhuth claimed him, and now enjoyed his "faithful continuance in well-doing" at their council board, where, as a leading member of the Unity's Elders' Conference—the highest authority of the Church,—he shared his mental gifts, as well in temporal as in spiritual necessities, for thirty years.

Endowed with natural energy of mind, his liberal edu cation, guarded and guided by the Spirit of God, perfected his usefulness at every point of his varied duties, whilst his unwavering faith in the power of God, and the truth of his word, was ever and anon the security of the boon of his lips, of which, however, I refer the reader to the "Life of Spangenberg," by Ledderhose.

He was not only professionally the coadjutor of Zinzendorff, but socially, his bosom friend: not blind to his faults, but of fervent charity, and a qualifying medium to any impetuosity that might escape his (Zinzendorff's) better judgment.

As the author of the "Life of Zinzendorff," he exhibits the virtues of his Christian profession, in the candid and impartial details of his life.

In this connection, Latrobe, in his preface to the above work, thus speaks of him:

"An individual more competent to the task, and altogether more worthy to execute it, could certainly not have been selected.

"With the exception of Zinzendorff himself, no name is more distinguished than that of Spangenberg in the records of the renewed Brethren's Church, and none more highly reverenced by its members. He was indeed a man of primitive piety and patriarchal simplicity, of extensive erudition, of unwearied diligence, and of unimpeachable veracity.

"The soundness and sobriety of his theological views are sufficiently proved by his well-known 'Exposition of Christian Doctrine,' and the variety and extent of his experience as a laborer in the vineyard of his Master, both at home and abroad, by his valuable tracts on subjects connected with the missionary calling; whilst the annals of the Brethren's Unity, during a period of nearly sixty years, have abundant testimony to the blessing vouchsafed to his truly apostolic labors."

His talents were not limited in his pen; the pulpit heralded his eloquence, and the people fed richly upon its fare, yet humility was his safeguard against flattery, and that charity that "vaunteth not itself, is not puffed up, and seeketh not her own," presented its defensive shield against the influence of any suggestion of the natural man.

For a more familiar address, he chose the name "Joseph," and "*Brother* Joseph" was the facile avenue to his notice, and "right hand of fellowship," during the greater part of his life.

But it is neither my province, my power, nor my promise, to *fill* a biography of the characters before me. I merely call up their manes, and present them as amongst the pious and untiring fathers of our Church.

Bishop Spangenberg slept with his fathers, on the 18th day of September, 1792, and his remains were deposited, on the 23d, in the burial-ground of the United Brethren Congregation, at Herrnhuth, in his 89th year.

PETER BOEHLER, EPISCOPUS.

"Let a man so account of us as of the ministers of Christ, and stewards of the mysteries of God" (1 Cor. 4 : 1); and, as such, we are happy to account also for this reverend brother.

Amongst the most vigorous servants of the Brethren's Church, we find this practical Brother Boehler, who, in addition to his piety, was rendered more variously available for the work before him, by a thorough education, logical and theological, in the University at Jena, a town of Saxe Weimar.*

His acquaintance with Count Zinzendorff began here; and their frequent intercourse won his affections, not only to the Count, but to his Church.

Conversant with its principles, and observant of the purity and zeal of its members, he enlisted under its banner, put on "the whole armor of God," and went forth to the work.

Already, in 1734, when but twenty-two years of age, and the tenth of the renewal of the Church, we find him preaching in London; and forming and fostering a Brethren's Society, in Gracehall, now Fulnec, the wedge of Moravianism in that quarter.

In 1735, he is the companion of Bishop Spangenberg, and the Reverends John and Charles Wesley, to Georgia,

* He was born, Dec. 31st, 1712, in Frankfort on the Maine.

PETRUS BOEHLER.

in North America, where he also spread the Lord's table. His acquaintance here with the Wesleys warmed to an interesting intimacy; so that in 1738, on his return to London, their associations included the Rev. George Whitfield there; and a profitable intercourse ensued. Differences of opinion, however, not so much doctrinal as dogmatical, divided their views. From this difference grew the powerful and thrifty Methodist Church, a happy issue to the world, for they too are a good and a godly people.

The Latin tongue must have been more familiar than his own vernacular, German, since he preached and prayed in that language, which was rendered into English afterwards, by the Rev. John Gambold, of the English Church, who subsequently joined the Brethren's Church, became eminent in divinity, and was furthered to the Episcopacy of that Church.

In 1746, Zinzendorff left him in charge of the affairs in Herrnhuth, during his sojourn elsewhere. And in 1748, he, too, was added to the Episcopate.

In 1756 to 1760, he was assistant to Bishop Spangenberg, in his supervision of the North American churches, and resided in Bethlehem, Pa., where he was identified with and much beloved by his people. In 1764, he was elected a member of the Directory, or Unity's Elders' Conference, sitting in Herrnhuth; but continued his labors in Bethlehem until 1774, when he retired to Herrnhuth; and there, on the 27th of April, 1775, departed this life, in the 63d year of his age.

Bishop Boehler was evidently a man of talent, available in his aptness to teach. His oratorical powers were beyond mediocrity, but were never drawn upon to smother the burden of his heart, whence sprang the endeavor to "persuade men." His ministration, therefore, was acceptable everywhere, and at all times; and his godliness "profitable unto all things."

His memory still floats on the atmosphere of Bethlehem and Nazareth, whilst the *life* of his character is yet in our ear, from the lips of those whose immediate embrace knew and felt from him what it was to be "kindly affectioned one to another." We, therefore, pass *his* manes to the respectful remembrance of the Christian world as a faithful "minister of Christ," and according to the requirement of St. Paul to Timothy, 1: 3, 7, "A man of good report from them that are without."

JOHN LEONHARD DOBER.

Episcopus.

LEONARD DOBER, EPISCOPUS.

"Out of the mouth of babes and sucklings hast thou ordained strength." (Ps. 8 : 2.)

At the coronation of Christian VI, of Denmark, in 1731, Count Zinzendorff being a guest in Copenhagen, he was called to baptize a negro into the Christian faith.

This convert, Anton, or Anthony, enlisted the sympathies of Zinzendorff for his heathen brethren in St. Thomas, where he had a sister, whose enlightenment and salvation he was even then sorrowing for "after a godly sort."

Immediately on his return to Herrnhuth, Zinzendorff made known this want to the congregation. Fired with holy zeal, Leonard Dober and Tobias Leupold, two spirited youths of the congregation, bosom friends, conceived, each for himself, a missionary spirit; nor did they open their minds to each other until the next day, when mutual surprise warmed their zeal to an immediate offer of their services.

Difficulties were pictured and obstacles multiplied before them, and even Anton, who was then in Herrnhuth, thought a breach in the bulwark impracticable, without becoming and working with the negroes as "slaves," the severity of whose duties, by day and by night, he fully set forth.

Nothing daunted, they accepted the terms, and urged their desire, until finally the word of the Lord came to them, through the lot, "Lasset den knaben ziehen der Herr ist mit ihm." "Let the youth go, for the Lord is with him."

Leupold, however, was detained, and David Nitchman appointed in his stead.

On their way to and at Copenhagen much dissuasion beset them, but "Go forward," was the impetus of their hearts, and the 13th of Dec. 1732, found them holding their "great light" over those who were "sitting in darkness," in the Island of St. Thomas.

In 1733, Brother Dober was left alone, by the recall to Herrnhuth of his co-arbiter, Nitchman; but finding favor with the overseer, was installed in his house as steward of his domestic economy, the duties of which however increasing, interfered with his missionary plan, and he was obliged to retire from that office, and take a small room for a residence. Here, cast upon his own resources, he hired himself as watchman for the inhabitants, and at the same time went to his trade, that of a potter; both of which, however, were not sufficiently lucrative to spread his table with a single condiment to his "bread and water;" but his happiness was not marred by this, so long as he could have access to the souls of his spiritual patients.

After feeling the influence of a six months' rebellion in St. John's, and planting the "mustard-seed" of faith, and enjoying a sight of its sprouts, he was relieved by his early friend Leupold and others, and called to Herrnhuth, in 1735, where he was appointed general superintendent of the spiritual department of the churches, which office he held till 1741.

From 1741 to 1747, he visited and sojourned amongst

many of the congregations in Europe, always to the profit of his recipients.

In 1747, he was consecrated a bishop of the Church, and continued his faithfulness to his Church, visiting and counselling his churches in different parts of Europe, until his "mortal was called to put on immortality," and the "crown of righteousness" was presented to his brow, as the reward of his "good fight of faith."

He was born in Munshroth, in Suabia, on the 7th of April, 1706; and departed this life on the 13th of April, 1766, in his 60th year, and interred at Hennersdorf, in Germany.

He was a man of firm decision, active and persevering, courageous in his religious pursuits, grave in deportment, but affable in social intercourse; always exemplifying that "godliness is profitable unto all things, having promise of the life that now is, and of that which is to come." (1 Tim. 4 : 8.)

CHRISTIAN DAVID, NON-EPISCOPUS.

"The sparrow hath found an house, and the swallow a nest for herself, even thine altars, O Lord of hosts." (Psalm 84 : 3.) With these words, fell the uplifted axe of this man of faith, upon the first tree that was smitten at Herrnhuth, to make way for the altar of the Lord, whence to exalt the valleys, make low the hills, and smooth the rough places that bestrode the way of evangelization.

This act of faith, of June 17, 1722, was blest and realized, in October of the same year, in the completion and consecration of the tabernacle; and Christian David, a grateful participant in the enjoyment, thanked God, took courage, and made known their wants in his prayer and supplication, at the conclusion of that most interesting ceremony.

He was a tie from the ancient to the renewed Church of the Brethren.

Emigrated from Moravia to Goerlitz, in 1717, where he was awakened under the Rev. M. Sharpe, after which, he returned to seek and gather up his countrymen, and restore them to the sanctuary.

He did return, and, like Noah's dove, wandered over the troubled waters of uncertainty and persecution, before the olive-branch peered over the storm, and offered itself as a voucher for peace.

Count Zinzendorff offered him an asylum on his estate,

CHRISTIAN DAVID.

Missionary.

at Berthlesdorf, whence grew a lovely union of spirit, and the "open door" that was set before him was not shut from the lifting of his axe at Herrnhuth, till his holy zeal had rained down spirit and power over the unwept ills of distant heathen soil, and the clod of the valley gave "peace to his ashes."

His frequent returns to his native country, to warn and warm up his brethren there, and his journeys into Bohemia, Switzerland, and Livonia, in behalf of his Church, are amongst the grateful recollections of the Brethren's Church, as they doubtless are to the Christian world in general.

But his undaunted courage, and self-sacrificing pursuit of souls in Greenland, are memorabilia worthy of a martyr.

In 1733, when the Christian world was young, and the moral world a wilderness, he joined "Brother Matthew Stach," and other heroes in the cause, in this hazardous enterprise; and although hunger, thirst, and murder itself, were pictured with all their terrors, as the fruit of their labors, their ardor was not softened, nor their zeal abated; they trusted in God, whom they believed had sent them, and said, "God, in the promotion of his kingdom on earth, has ever operated with small and unsightly materials, to show that to Him alone belongs the glory, and to teach man that he only must give the increase."

Again, when in Copenhagen, on their way to the work, Count Pleiss, a gentleman who was much interested in them, asked them how they intended to procure a livelihood? Unacquainted with the situation and climate of the country, they replied, "By the labor of our hands, and God's blessing;" adding, that they would build houses, and cultivate a piece of land. Being told that there was no wood in that region, they said, "We will dig holes in the earth, and lodge there."

The Count, astonished at their ardor, gave them fifty dollars to buy timber there, and take with them for the construction of a house.

They went, the mission was set, and their labors were blest.

Always alive to the duties of a Christian missionary, and unscathed of his early affections—after many intermediate migrations—he returned to his spiritual garden in Greenland, in 1747, to confirm his covenant with its growth, in the superintendence of the erection of a Church at New Herrnhuth, and in 1749, again to conduct some Greenland converts to their home.

His wonted residence was Herrnhuth, where, when not engaged officially, he "labored with his hands," at his trade as carpenter.

Episcopal orders were not conferred upon him, being neither craved by ambition, nor necessary to his spiritual might; for, as he wielded the axe at Herrnhuth,* in the beginning, so, throughout his life, did he wield "the sword of the Spirit," severing the cords that bound the heathen, to "the world, the flesh, and the devil," in its passes among heathen nations.

* Herrnhuth, not generally understood, is thus translated and explained, in Holmes' History of the United Brethren, p. 169.

"It has a double signification, and may be translated, either the object of the Lord's protection, or the watch of the Lord, the place where his servants stand waiting, to receive and execute his commands."

This place shall be called "the watch of the Lord (des Hut des Herrn"), was Christian David's solution, &c. &c.

Without any pretensions to refinement in oratory, spirit and power were in his utterance, whilst his biblical knowledge always lit up his "pictures of silver, with apples of gold," whose impress yet marks the fields of his spiritual culture.

Count Zinzendorff said of him, at his funeral discourse, that "the Bible was so precious to him, that he never tired in its perusal. He was never idle, but whatever his hands found to do, he did with all his might. If once convinced that he was undertaking anything according to the will of his Lord, and for the good of his neighbor, he did not suffer himself to be hindered by any difficulties in the way of its execution."

He was born in Senftleben, in Moravia, December 31st, 1690, and departed this life on the 3d of February, 1754.

DAVID NITCHMAN, EPISCOPUS.

Consecrated Bishop of the Brethren's Church, in 1735.

"For you see your calling, brethren, how that not many. wise men after the flesh, not many mighty, not many noble, are called.

"But God hath chosen the foolish things of the world to confound the wise, and God hath chosen the weak things of the world to confound the things that are mighty." 1 Cor. 1 : 26, 27.

Here we have a shining light upon this dogma of the Apostle Paul.

David Nitchman was by trade a carpenter, as was his father before him.

He was born in Zauchenthal, Moravia, in 1696, was a member of the ancient Brethren's Church, and as a remnant of that, was a pioneer in its resuscitation and an ardent, fearless, and devoted colaborer in the work of the Gospel of Jesus Christ.

He was one of the five brethren who laid their axe at the root of the pride of the forest, in order to plant a tree of perennial beauty, whose leaves should be "for the healing of the nations;" and to this end was a witness and aid to the laying of the corner-stone of the first church in Herrnhuth, on the 12th of May, 1724.

In 1732, he accompanied Brother Leonard Dober to the Island of St. Thomas, for the purpose of establishing a mission, or, at all events, to break up the fallow

David Nitschmann

First Bishop of the Brethren's Church.

Born Decr 27th 1696. Died October 8th 1772.

ground of the benighted negroes; but after a year of opening there, was recalled to Herrnhuth, 1733, for local purposes.

In 1735, he was consecrated the first Bishop of the Moravian—renewed—Church, by Bishop Jablonsky and the Polish Moravian Bishop Sitkovius, and also assisted as Episcopus with Bishop Jablonsky at the consecration to the Episcopacy of Count Zinzendorff, in 1737.

In 1740, he was a party to the beginning of the village of Nazareth, in Pennsylvania, and in the spring of 1741, was a like party to the founding of the head-quarters of the Church, in Bethlehem, Pennsylvania.

Here, with Bishop Spangenberg and others, he was appointed supervisor of the several settlements of the Brethren, acting either in concert or succession, as necessity required. He was upwards of seventy years of age at the beginning of this work. Yet, undaunted by fear or infirmity, he yielded to none in trust in God for a successful issue.

The corner-stone at Herrnhuth was, under God, the anchor of his hope for Bethlehem.

Although wasting in bodily strength under the deepening shades of time, his mental energies, imbued from his youth, grew on in the things that belonged to his and the eternal peace of his Indian flocks, in Pennsylvania, with whose missionaries he kept a lively, interesting, and profitable correspondence unto his last end, which time and the grace of God guarded until the 4th of April, 1758, giving him eighty-one years of sojourn on earth.

A persevering self-sacrificing Christian, of indomitable zeal, earnest and determined in the cause of his Master, unterrified by the perils of the sea, and unconcerned for he threats of poverty and want on land.

His "staff and stay" were neither purse nor scrip, but "the kingdom of God and its righteousness" was the field of his labors, and the soil that was to add all else to him, and this he cultivated in his fifty voyages, from point to point, incurring "the perils of the sea," weariness, painfulness, and frequent watching, all with untiring zeal in the holy cause of his espousal.

ERDMUTH DOROTHEA COUNTESS ZINZENDORF

Born Novr 7th 1700, Died June 9th 1756.

THE COUNTESS ERDMUTH DOROTHEA VON ZINZENDORFF.

THE memory of this "mother in Israel" has just claims upon our pen, not merely as the spouse of the well-born and pious youth of Dresden, nor the silken cord of the matrimonial tie with a titled gentleman, nor yet as a titled lady and figurante in the world of startling events, but as one devoted to the cause of Christ and his Church, divesting herself of the privileges open to her rank, eschewing the fascinations of a gay and solicitous circle, and rejecting the insidious presence of the captivating influences of the gay world.

She adopted her husband's views, and was at once a "handmaid" to him in his varied and laborious undertakings; aiding and furthering his spiritual designs, and, at the same time, guarding the means and the measures escaping too rapidly from his liberal treasury; for, although Zinzendorff did not "spend his money for that which is nought," it is well known, that "self-preservation was not *his* first law of nature."

Holmes, in his "History of the Protestant Church of the United Brethren," speaks of her as follows:

"In reference to her union with Count Zinzendorff, it is not sufficient to say that she discharged, with Christian fidelity, all the duties of a wife, mother, and mistress of her family, but she entered into all his views for the propagation of the Gospel, and became his faithful coadjutrix in his labors in the Brethren's Church, gladly sharing in the reproach he suffered for the name of Christ.

"When, for the Gospel's sake, he relinquished all his expectations of wealth and worldly honor, and subjected himself to banishment and persecutions; instead of repining at her loss, as the world would call it, she accounted it gain to suffer the loss of all things, that she might win Christ.

"Instead of harassing her consort by grieving and murmuring, she confirmed him in his resolutions, and encouraged his faith and trust in God.

"When he was disqualified from attending to his temporal concerns, she took the whole management of his estates, as well as of his domestic affairs, into her hands.

"Though of a delicate constitution, and the mother of twelve children, she accompanied her husband on many of his journeys and voyages, or bore repeated and long separations from him, without repining, whenever they were rendered necessary in the vineyard of Christ.

"In short, they were one heart and soul, not only in their conjugal relations, but in their determination to consecrate themselves, their children, their time, and their wealth, to Christ and his service."

This may suffice to show that "she was a lady of no common endowments; and perhaps the only one who in every respect could have so completely adapted herself to the peculiar situation in which she was placed, by her marriage, and the vocation of her consort."

She was the sister of Count Henry Reuss, an intimate

associate of Count Zinzendorff, to whom she was married on the 7th of September, 1722; and departed this life in the month of June (19th), 1756, in the 56th year of her age. On the 25th, her remains were interred in the burial-ground of the church at Herrnhuth, largely, solemnly, and tearfully attended.

CHAPTER XXXIII.

Conclusion—Table of the Episcopate, &c.

HAVING thus brought to view a portraiture of a few of the early and very efficient heads and leaders of the *Unitas Fratrii*, not, however, as a boastful show of their prowess, nor even as a guarantee for the doings of their successors; for, however true it be, that the Moravian Church of the present, is an active principle, and a doctrinal succession of its fathers, yet we cannot deny the difference of the practical *minutiæ* of this, compared with that "day of small things."

Simplicity of word and deed, and even faith itself, have passed into and through the refining fire of the march of improvement; and "the spirit of the age," offers them in a cruder form.

That there is a deterioration of the manners, customs, profession, and practical illustration of the religion of our Saviour, is beyond controversy. And why? Are we any better than they? Are we as powerful and successful? Certainly not. But we refine too much of God's holy Word, make it enigmatical; and the plain, simplified effusions of our Saviour's mind are mystified in figures of speech. He said, "If ye have faith as a grain of mustard-seed, and shall say to this sycamore tree, Be thou removed, and cast into the sea, it shall be done." And he proved it when by an act of the same faith, he, at the marriage at Cana, turned water into wine.

It was upon this surety—divesting themselves entirely of self-dependence—that our fathers lived and moved and had their ministerial being. And but for this, all the sacrifices in the world could not have wrought the successful issues to the work of their hands.

They were plain simple-hearted men, unsophisticated, ungarnished of worldly wisdom, having only "a single eye to the glory of God," believing, that as Jesus Christ "is the same yesterday, to-day, and forever," so the faith inculcated and founded upon his eternity, was as good a foundation for *their* superstruction as it was to the more immediate recipients of the instruction.

They went forth "without purse or scrip," with trust in God for their treasury, and faith their luminary to the point of their pursuit, and manned them for the perils of their enterprise.

Now, may we not ask, where is this practical faith nowadays? And who will believe our report if we show some of these men almost miraculously fed in the wilderness? And yet the history of the Moravian Missions, by "Rister," gives a remarkable instance of this "substance of things hoped for."

The distance from Bethlehem to the Iroquois Nations was great, and perilous to pass; highways were few, and byways and paths through dense forests the only alternative to the missionary; moreover, it was impossible for them to carry provisions for a journey of three months, especially being on foot.

On one of these occasions, when about to encamp for the night in a wood, by the side of a stream, the Brethren

Spangenberg, Zeisberger, and Schebosh found themselves without food.

The Bishop (Spangenberg) requested Zeisberger to cast his net and catch fish. The latter, smiling, said to his companion, "Spangenberg does not know much about fishing," and turning to him said, "There are no fish here; the water is muddy and cold, and the fish have gone to the bottom."

The Bishop repeated his command; the net was cast, and the abundance required the power of two of them to secure. After their repast, they dried the surplus for future use; but in process of days, they again fell short, and were again supplied by the haunch of a bear, left by the Indians hanging on a tree before them.

We might present very many instances of answers to the prayer of faith, but the difference between the simplicity of these fathers in their literal conceptions of Holy Writ, and the sons of the present day, is, alas! too great to spare the details, the obloquy of fabulous reports; notwithstanding, they are a part of the riches of history, and by which we thank God that we can say, these elders obtained "a good report."

We do not mean to hold up these men merely as Moravians; for, doubtless, there were others equally bound up by this silken tie to "the secrets of the Lord;" but as ensamples to induce and encourage ourselves to turn from the byways of mystified construction, and, like Elias, pass direct to the brow of the hill, and pray for rain, and get it.

Eschewing bigotry in any form, it is, however, but common justice to the Moravian Church to say, that it was a seed pregnant of faith, fructified by faithfulness, and rich in its bearing, and that the practical faith of its fathers will compare with anything in religion, from the days of the Apostles; but we would not offer *their* sunset as a repose to their generations, nor as a salvo to the manifest difference between their doings and ours. And why this? Is faith not the same? Is the promise not the same? Is God's requirement not the same? Yea, "let God be true, and every man a liar;" they are all the same; but where are we? Compromising faith, to meet the spirit of the age; whilst religious epicurianism is in general but too easily satisfied with the paling shadows of the memory of the fathers of the faithful.

> "Return, O Holy Dove, return,
> Sweet messenger of rest;
> I hate the sins that make thee mourn,
> And drove thee from my breast."

As matter of general history, I append the following from "The Moravian," of May 30th, 1856, as arranged by the Rev. E. A. De Schweinitz, pastor of the Church in Philadelphia, and one of the editors of that very valuable organ of the Church.

THE EPISCOPAL SUCCESSION IN THE MORAVIAN CHURCH, FROM THE YEAR 1467 TO THE YEAR 1856.

The second column shows the years in which the Bishops were consecrated, the fourth column contains explanatory remarks. The word "Praeses" means that the Bishop, aside of whose name it stands, was the *senior Bishop* (as to the time of consecration), primus inter pares, whose prerogative it was to preside at the Synods. The ancient Unity was divided into the Moravian, Bohemian, and Polish branches. In the list of Bishops of the Renewed Church, the words "N. America, England," &c., signify that the Bishops aside of whose names they stand, held or hold official stations in those countries.

Ancient Church.

Nos.	Year of Ordination.	Bishops.	Remarks.
1.	1467.	Michael Bradacius,	Praeses.
2.	"	A Waldensian pastor who had joined the Brethren.	
3.	"	A Roman Catholic priest who had joined the Brethren.	
4.	"	Matthias of Kunewalde,	Praeses.
5.	"	Procopius,	Praeses for 27 years.
6.	1499.	Thomas Prälauzius,	Praeses for 11 years.
7.	"	Elias Chrzenovius.	
8.	1503.	Lucas of Prague,	Praeses for 10 years.
9.	"	Ambrosius Skutecensis.	
10.	1506.	Wenceslaus.	
11.	"	Daniel.	
12.	1516.	Martinus Szkoda,	Praeses for 5 years.
13.	1529.	Wenceslaus Albus.	
14.	"	Andreas Ciclovius.	
15.	"	John Horn,	Praeses for 15 years.
16.	1532.	Benedictus Bavorinus.	
17.	"	Vitus Michalecius.	
18.	"	John Augusta,	Praeses for 25 years.
19.	1537.	Martinus Michalecius.	
20.	"	Matthias Sionius.	
21.	1550.	John Czerny.	
22.	"	Matthias.	
23.	"	Paul Paulinus.	
24.	1553.	Matthias Czervenka.	
25.	1557.	George Israel,	Praeses in Poland for 16 years.
26.	"	John Blahoslav.	
27.	1571.	Andreas Stephanus.	
28.	"	John Caleph,	Praeses in Moravia for 6 months.
29.	"	John Laurentius.	
30.	1577.	Zacharias Litomislensis,	Praeses for 2 years.
31.	"	John Æneas,	Praeses for 4 years.
32.	1587.	John Abdias.	

Nos.	Year of Ordination.	Bishops.	Remarks.
33.	1587.	Simon Turnovius,	Praeses in Poland for 14 years.
34.	1589.	John Ephraim.	
35.	"	Paul Jessenius.	
36.	1594.	Jacob Narcissus,	Praeses for 3 years.
37.	"	John Niemczanius.	
38.	1599.	Samuel Sussicius.	
39.	"	Zacharias Ariston.	
40.	1601.	Bartholomew Niemczanius.	
41.	"	John Lanecius,	Praeses for 15 years.
42.	1606.	John Cruciger.	
43.	1608.	Martin Gertichius,	Praeses in Poland for 3 years.
44.	"	Matthias Rybinius.	
45.	1609.	Matthias Koneczny.	
46.	1611.	Matthias Cyrus.	
47.	1612.	John Turnovius,	Praeses in Poland for 30 days.
48.	"	Gregory Erastus,	Praeses in Bohemia for 14 years.
49.	1618.	John Cyrillus.	
50.	1627.	Daniel Micolajevius.	
51.	1629.	Paul Paliurus.	
52.	1632.	Laurentius Justinus,	Praeses in Bohemia and Moravia for 5 years.
53.	"	Matthias Procopius.	
54.	"	Amos Comenius,	Praeses for 23 years. The last Bishop of the Bohemian Moravian branch; the rest are all Bishops of the Polish branch.
55.	"	Paul Fabricius.	
56.	1633.	Martin Orminius.	
57.	"	John Rybinius.	
58.	1644.	Martin Gertichius, Jun.	
59.	"	John Büttner.	
60.	1662.	Nicholas Gertichius.	

Nos.	Year of Ordination.	Bishops.	Remarks.
61.	1662.	Peter Jablonsky.	
62.	1673.	Adam S. Hartman.	
63.	1676.	John Zugehör.	
64.	1692.	Joachim Gulich.	
65.	1699.	John Jacobides.	
66.	"	Dan. Ernst Jablonsky.	
67.	1709.	Solomon Opitz.	
68.	1712.	David Cassius.	
69.	1725.	Paul Cassius.	
70.	1734.	Christian Sitkovius.	

Renewed Church.

Nos.	Year of Ordination.	Bishops.	Remarks.
71.	1735.	David Nitschman,	N. America.
72.	1737.	Lewis Count Zinzendorff.	
73.	1740.	Polycarp Müller.	
74.	1741.	John Nitschman, Sen.	
75.	1743.	Frederick de Watteville.	
76.	1744.	Martin Dober.	
77.	1745.	Augustus G. Spangenberg,	N. America.
78.	1746.	David Nitschman, Jun.	
79.	"	Frederick W. Neisser.	
80.	"	Christian F. Steinhofer.	
81.	"	J. F. Camerhof,	N. America.
82.	1747.	John de Watteville.	
83.	"	Leonhard Dober.	
84.	"	A. A. Vieroth.	
85.	1748.	Frederick Martin,	W. Indies.
86.	"	Peter Bœhler,	N. America.
87.	1750.	G. Waiblinger.	
88.	1751.	Matthew Hehl,	N. America.
89.	1754.	John Gambold,	England.
90.	1756.	A. Grasman.	
91.	1758.	John Nitschman.	
92.	"	Nath. Seidel,	N. America.
93.	1770.	Martin Mack,	W. Indies.
94.	1773.	M. Graf,	N. America.

Nos.	Year of Ordination.	Bishops.	Remarks.
95.	1775.	J. F. Reichel.	
96.	"	P. E. Layritz.	
97.	"	P. H. Molther.	
98.	1782.	H. de Brueningk.	
99.	"	G. Clemens.	
100.	"	Jeremiah Risler.	
101.	1783.	Geo. Tranecker.	
102.	1784.	John Etwein,	N. America.
103.	1785.	John Schaukirch,	N. America.
104.	1786.	B. G. Müller.	
105.	1789.	Christian Gregor.	
106.	"	Samuel Liebisch.	
107.	"	C. Duvernoy.	
108.	"	Benj. Rothe.	
109.	1790.	J. A. Huebner,	N. America.
110.	"	J. D. Kœhler,	N. America.
111.	1801.	Thomas Moore,	England.
112.	"	Christian Dober.	
113.	"	S. T. Benade,	England.
114.	"	Gotthold Reichel,	N. America.
115.	1802.	G. H. Loskiel,	N. America.
116.	1808.	J. G. Cunow.	
117.	"	Herman Richter.	
118.	1811.	John Herbst,	N. America.
119.	1814.	W. Fabricius.	
120.	"	C. G. Hueffel,	N. America.
121.	"	C. A. Baumeister.	
122.	"	J. B. de Albertini.	
123.	1815.	Jacob Van Vleck,	N. America.
124.	1818.	G. M. Schneider.	
125.	"	F. W. Foster,	England.
126.	"	Benjamin Reichel.	
127.	1822.	Andrew Benade,	N. America.
128.	1825.	Hans Wied.	
129.	"	Lewis Fabricius.	
130.	"	P. F. Curie.	
131.	"	John Holmes,	England.

Nos.	Year of Ordination.	Bishops.	Remarks.
132.	1827.	J. D. Anders,	N. America.
133.	1835.	Fred. L. Kœlbing.	
134.	"	John C. Bechler,	N. America.
135.	1836.	C. A. Pohlman.	
136.	"	H. P. Halbeck,	S. Africa.
137.	"	Jacob Levin Reichel.	
138.	"	D. F. Gambs.	
139.	"	Wm. Henry Van Vleck,	N. America.
140.	"	John K. Martyn,	England.
141.	"	John Ellis,	W. Indies.
142.	1843.	John M. Nitschman.	
143.	"	C. C. Ultsch.	
144.	"	John Stengärd.	
145.	1844.	W. Wisdom Essex,	England.
146.	1845.	Peter Wolle,	N. America.
147.	1846.	J. G. Herman,	N. America.
148.	"	Benj. Seifferth,	England.
149.	1848.	C. W. Matthiesen.	
150.	1852.	F. Joachim Nielsen,	St. Petersburg, Russia.
151.	"	John Rogers,	England.
152.	1853.	J. C. Breutel.	
153.	"	Henry T. Dober.	
154.	"	George Wall Westerby,	W. Indies.
155.	1854.	John C. Jacobson,	N. America.

Of these Bishops the following thirteen are living:

Andrew Benade,	The senior Bishop of the whole Unity, living in retirement at Bethlehem, Pa. He has been a Bishop for 34 years.
John C. Bechler,	Living in retirement at Herrnhuth, Saxony.
John Martin Nitschman,	Member of the Unity's Elders' Conference, and President of the same.
Christian W. Matthiesen,	Member of do.
John C. Breutel,	Member of do.
Henry T. Dober,	Stationed at Gnadenfeld, in Silesia.
Christian C. Ultsch,	Stationed at Gnadenfrei, in Silesia.

John C. Jacobson,	Member of the Provincial Elders' Conference on the Northern Province of the American Church, and President of the same.
Peter Wolle,	Member of do.
Benjamin Seifferth.	Member of the British Provincial Helpers' Conference, and President of the same.
John Rogers,	Stationed at Fairfield, England.
George Wall Westerby,	Stationed on the island of Antigua.
F. J. Nielsen,	Stationed in St. Petersburg, Russia.

APPENDIX.

DIAGRAPH OF THE IMMEDIATE NEIGHBORHOOD OF THE OLD CHURCH,

FROM THE DATE OF ITS ORIGIN TO THE BEGINNING OF THE PRESENT CENTURY.

CHAPTER I.

A Glimpse of the Early Settlement, or Immediate Environs of the First Moravian Church, with Recollections of the Tenants in Common of that and after-time from the Church to Second Street, southward to Drinker's Alley, and northward to the Southeast Corner.

Although the history of this Church may have little to do with the history of Philadelphia, yet the city must adopt it as its own kith and kin, and share its dignity and the honors due to the antiquity of an important, though unpretending contributor to its rise and progress; for, in thus presenting herself, remoulded from the dust of oblivion, her comparative claims upon the march of improvement entitle her to a share of its respectful considerations, whilst the social circle of her centre may offer its radii to weld the venerable links of the olden time, or warm up the curiosity of rising generations.

To this end, from the fragments of data, the dew drops of memory, and the incontrovertible landmarks of tenacious facts, I shall gather and offer a retrospect of the vicinage of our Church, and that part of our now great city (then struggling with prosperity) for a modicum of its furtherance.

That Philadelphia was in its infancy in the year 1741, and for some years after, is certainly beyond controversy, and that the original Moravian Church was very near its western boundary, can be no less entitled to credulity.

Imagination, therefore, need not be severely taxed to see roads instead of streets, and paths instead of paves, as the conveniences for passing from point to point; nor to see west of Third Street a highway, to and from the city; whilst Allen's lot may have been bounded by a dusty or a muddy passage from Race to Arch Streets, erst brought into municipal notice by the title of the Church, that formed its southeast corner. There is, however, some data, for the dots and lines that constituted the life of this vicinage.

That Frederick II, King of Prussia, guarded the domains for the "entertainment of man and horse," *vis-à-vis* the Church, and that his sturdy equestrian figure was the beacon to the wayworn traveller, announcing its whereabouts, as it swung to the breeze, and creaked the pæans of the host within, for full three-quarters of a century, is scarcely matter of controversy, since, for nearly threescore of those years, the writer can vouch.

This tavern—for there were no hotels in those days—was kept, in 1795, by Abraham Butz; after him by a certain Peter Paris; and, subsequently, by Jacob Smith, in 1816. Its very extensive grounds on the rear, accessible by a ten or twelve feet passage from Race Street, was an inviting harbor for the retirement of horses, carriages, and vehicles of all sorts, and was extensively patronized.

Immediately west of this, was the store of Abraham Piesch* — a Swiss — an importer and large dealer in German goods, but afterwards an eminent shipping-merchant, and very successful in the West India carrying trade, when our superabundance of apples, onions,

* Under the firm of Piesch & Mayerhoff.

soap, candles, lard, &c. &c., went out at a *minimum*, and came back in coffee, often in bulk,—being superabundant there—and yielding a *maximum* here to every successive enterprise. Extending his sphere, however, the war of 1812 caught him, as well in Europe as on the high seas. Where, in the one case, his employees played false, and in the other the common enemy not only stopped his career by blockade and embargo, but enforced their rights of seizure according to the laws of war; and made this theretofore successful and highly respected merchant a bankrupt, and threw him into the chilling stream of poverty, and under the withering scowl of those who, in his prosperity, had bowed the knee to his purse; but now, alas! gave the cold shoulder to his person. Alas! alas! such is the horrible influence of dollars and cents. Whether honestly obtained or not, or lost by waste, extravagance, or dire misfortune, 'tis all the same; *the almighty dollar only* can lift the hat, or lubricate the knee. But to my subject.

In order, however, to present a more intelligible diagraph, I shall return to my centre, starting eastward from the church, taking a review of Race Street from Second to Third, with a sufficient scope at each turn to make up an historical boundary.

Proceeding, therefore, eastward, we have first the old red frame store-house* of 1785, then in the occupancy of John Peters, at £50 per annum; Jacob Lawersweiler, at £25; Godfrey Haga, at £15; in 1801, by C. Helmbold and John Geyer, printers; and finally, by George Ritter as a cabinet-maker's shop till 1810, when it was demolished, and a three-story brick put up in its place,* which,

* This building cost $1996 46.

being in the interior unfinished, was let to Charles Pommer as a piano manufactory, in which he established a good reputation for his instruments, and profited by the result.

This building was subsequently finished for a dwelling, and as such, was first occupied by the late George W. Mentz.

Adjoining this, there was a two-story faded-blue frame, occupied by Sukey Beck, widow of Jacob Beck, shoemaker, who sold cakes and spruce beer, but who was associated with shoe-making, or shoe-vending, as indicated by the two or three pairs of ready-made shoes arranged on a shelf, jutting from the sill of the window.

Sukey deserves a tribute to her memory for her very good-natured services at her counter, especially when we—boys—behaved to her satisfaction; but when we were naughty, and dripped the dregs of our cup in her face, as she ascended from the cellar through the trap door, behind the counter, the ordinary vocabulary—to her—was of minor importance.

Another two-story blue frame, of twelve feet front, was the residence, and pastry and fancy cake bakery of Mrs. Elizabeth Mentz, whose skill, tact, and talent, in that refined department of the culinary art, begat for her a profitable reputation, a respectable patronage, and a happy contribution to her domestic comforts.

The venerable Joseph North, a relic of much earlier times, occupied the next house, a two-story brick, with attic and dormer windows. It was about twenty-five feet front, door between the windows, and penthouse for protection of the lower front.

The Misses North, his sisters, kept a dry goods store there, before and after his demise.

Next to this, there was a very narrow and very aged two-story brick house, occupied, before this century, by a Mrs. Roderfield, as a fancy millinery, 1795; and in 1801, by Andrew Barnes, a shopkeeper.

A narrow passage here, running south, was the avenue to several small tenements, one of which was a school-house for children.

At the lower corner of this alley, there was a dirty yellow frame, standing some four or five feet from the line, occupied by a female as a huckster shop; who, not being famed for very tidy habits, fell heir to the soubriquet of "Dirty Nancy."*

The adjoining tenements were two three-story bricks, of ancient date—yet standing; the first was occupied by Mrs. Seitz, a widow lady, there resident for many years. The other was the residence and industrial department of Matthias (commonly called "Mattes") and John Roush, leather breeches makers, of whom a respectful reflex can neither be considered impious nor impertinent; and, therefore, to throw off, for the moment, our threescore, and wave the hat of our juvenility to these ancient friends, —for so they were in the year 1800—as at noon, or even-tide, they dignified their inviting porch, and listlessly acknowledged the passing nod, is but to cull a flower from the verdant field of our youthful ramblings, and offer it to the gatherings of antiquarian lore, with a respectful remembrance of our city's early fathers.

They were pioneers of that neighborhood, John Roush

* All of the above properties have passed their ordeal, and the ground is now occupied by two large stores, built by Conrad Grove, and constitute his mart for the sale of oils.

having occupied the corner frame, as skin-dresser, before 1795; as was well proven by the dark, dull, and almost obliterated sign of a pair of leather breeches, astraddle, fast fading to nonenity, yet catching the eye and winning the patronage of passers, for its industrious owners.

They were bachelors, well dried, and perhaps well *tried*, too, in the tandem of single blessedness; who, whilst their sunken lips lay buried between their nose and chin, the antique board over their door bore incontrovertible evidence of its contemporaneous services to the ways and means of their wear and tear.

Now coming to the southwest corner of Race and Second Street, we have another ante-revolutionary relic, in a two-story frame, occupied by Cadet Bergusse, as a fancy trimming and jobbing store; theretofore, by Isaac Roush, shopkeeper, in 1795. Proceeding southward, we have a certain John Rupp, or Roop, a shuster; Philip Heyl, a baker, No. 106; and next, No. 104, the active and highly intelligent Charles Cist, a Russian by birth, of St. Petersburg, a printer, *more by occupation than by trade;* a highly educated gentleman, of very wiry motion, but unmistakable intellect. Conrad Zentler afterwards occupied the premises, and thence issued the far-famed German Almanac, with its motto, "Wir leben in hoffnung besseren zeiten;"* heralded by an angel in flight, with a trumpet to its lips.

Poor man, his motto outlived and mocked his hopes; he died unsung by the reality, unwept by fortune, but not untold by fame. He was as notorious for his love of snuff, as he was for the proprietary of the "Amerikanishe Kalender."

* We live in hope of better times.

Mr. Zentler, by industry and economy, had gathered a moderate competency for the comforts due to declining life; and, for the better security of his purpose, invested it all in United States Bank stock; the failure of which denuded him of his protective mantle,—a convincing evidence that "It is not in man that walketh to direct his steps." (Jeremiah 10 : 23.)

Passing Caspar Graff, Jun., tailor, No. 100; Abraham Steinberg, shopkeeper, No. 98—since, the famous restaurant of James Lecount—and Daniel Boehm, grocer, &c., at 96; these—except Lecount, who went there in 1835—were of and previous to 1795.

Here we come to our present Quarry Street,* obliterating every vestige of domestic scenes, comforts, or conveniences; but history, Time's hand-maid, gathers up the dust, and remoulds the very large three-story brick mansion and residence of Thomas Bartow—a highly respectable merchant of his day, 1791—and probably so early as 1785, at the time of his active and efficient services in the Moravian Church, and fills that gap.

In 1795, it was the centre of busier scenes, when George Lesher's stage-office offered a swiftsure to Bethlehem; and his "Jehus" cracked their whips or blew their horns in announcement of their readiness, or as a proud earnest of their speed and promptness; but the tale of woe came after; it was often a three days' journey—now, a flight of three hours.

* Quarry Street, originally, was laid out and opened from Third Street, running eastward only to Moravian Alley. The title and right of soil of the land in this compass, was in a certain Sarah Quarry, who, in 1716, devised it by will to certain heirs; the derivative of Quarry Street, I think, may therefore be safely traced to this ownership.

Again we pass the mercantile location of Josiah Willard and William Gibbs, and the dwelling of Josiah Willard Gibbs, probably the same who was in mercantile pursuits, about forty years ago, as J. W. Gibbs, at the northwest corner of Greenleaf Court, now Merchant Street, in Fourth below Market Street.

Here we come to a pile venerable for its antiquity, respectable for its appearance, and historical for its services.

This was a two story double front brick mansion, parlors or rooms at each side of the hall, or front entrance.

The house was set some six or eight feet from the line, and the lot extended from Second Street to Moravian Alley, some two hundred feet in depth, and was the garden of the mansion.

Some time previous to 1740, it was occupied by the Governor of the province.

In 1742, it was the residence of John Stephen Benezet, known to history as a Huguenot refugee.

He was born in Abbeville, France, June 22d, 1683, was the father of James, Philip, Daniel, and Anthony Benezet, (of whom Daniel was the father of Mrs. Sarah Bartow,) a gentleman of wealth, and carriage convenience, who, apprehensive of British thirst for booty, in the revolutionary war,—buried his silver plate, of which he had an abundance, in his cellar, and threw an old stove-plate over the secret, which guarded it till danger fled with its cause.

Some of this plate is now in the possession of his granddaughter, Mrs. Wm. S. Crothers, of this city, and of the Horsefield family of Bethlehem.

His son Anthony, was, perhaps, the greatest philanthropist of the age, and too well known to history for me to attempt to illuminate. He had chosen the Society of Friends for his religious home, and, if they will admit of such a thing, was an ornament of that body.

The sire of this issue, John Stephen, was a member of Christ Church, whose Prayer Book is even now in good preservation, in the hands of his generation of the fourth part, Wm. S. son of the above-named Mrs. Crothers.

I am thus particular, in my details of the advent and issues of this gentleman, because of his hospitalities to Zinzendorff, his evident faith in his creed and religious purposes, and his furtherance of these purposes, in opening his doors for the gatherings and religious services of his little band, besides entertaining him as a guest. Mr. B. had formed the acquaintance of Peter Boehler, and his efforts in London, appreciated their operations, and therefore, advisedly gave to Zinzendorff, "the right hand of fellowship."

De Watteville and Whitfield were also recipients of the rites of hospitality at his hands. He must have been a Christian brother.

Moreover, as matter of physiological fact, in him we have the germ of that benevolence which appears to have been perfected in his son Anthony, and which covered poverty and discomfort with wide-spread wings of love, and efficient human sympathy; nor do I mean to confine this Christian virtue to that sphere, seeing that Mrs. Sarah Bartow, niece of Anthony, well known to me in my youth, was of a like spirit, and a most exemplary member of the Moravian Church. "By their fruits ye shall know them;" and they were favorably known, from the stem even to the outer branches.

This mansion, No. 90 North Second Street, was occupied by Jacob Lawerswyler, for many years after. He was a sugar refiner, more tritely called in those days a sugar baker, and had his sugar house on the rear of his lot, fronting on Moravian Alley.

The east side of Second Street has lost less of its identity than the west side, seeing that north of Drinker's Alley several ancient three-story brick houses remain; and even south of it, there is a fair show of old times.

But there was a thing of life, living and being in an upper appartment of a house near Race Street, a certain Ernest L. Bisch, a miser of note, 1793 to 1795.

He had—by means known only to himself—accumulated a great deal of money, utterly useless, except for its shine upon his avarice, and its nutritive offerings to a most depraved and ungodly appetite for "filthy lucre."

He went forth every day, and returned to his haunt at eventide, but neither food nor fuel was ever known to pass his threshold.

But "all things to their period bend." His sortie ceased; the snow at his entrance no longer bore his impress; curiosity was startled; "wonder grew;" all of which combined, smote his door, and the secret stared them blank, of course, in the face.

Bisch was dead on the stairs, on his way upwards, with a death-grasp of the banisters! Dead to the world and all his heart held dear!

Report told of coin, gold and silver, hid in every nook, corner, and crevice of his room. Here, then, was "the love of money, the root of all evil."

Next above, William Rogers, a very clever Irish gentleman, kept a grocery store, in a two-story frame building;

and at the southeast corner of Race and Second, a Mrs. Hedricks kept a boarding house.

Peter Paris, of the King of Prussia tavern, after Mrs. Hedricks, owned and occupied the house as a private residence, and subsequently, about the year 1802, his son-in-law, William Spohn, made a grocery business stand of it, and, as such, furthered his occupation.*

This corner, and several adjoining houses, have been recently torn down; and even now—April, 1857—the vacancy awaits the order of the day.

* William Spohn had been of the firm of Hahn & Spohn, who had been established at the northwest corner of Front and Arch Streets; and, in process of history, it may not be amiss to state here, that this corner was formerly the counting-house of James C. & Samuel W. Fisher, which, with several of the neighboring estates, are yet in the possession of the Fisher family.

CHAPTER II.

Continuance of Comparative View from the Southeast Corner of Second and Race Street, East and West Side of Second, to New Street, and North Side of Race to Third Street.

The northeast corner of Second and Race Street was, perhaps, originally built up of brick, three stories, and, far from the present century, occupied by Christian Wirtz, the father-in-law of the sire of the present generation of the Wager family, Philip Wager, the elder.

Next above, also, a brick house was the starting-point of Abraham Wilt, the elder, in the oil business.

Next above this, Mrs. Desilver and her sister, Miss Jane Owen, kept a very respectable dry goods store, which was as respectably patronized.

The late Henry Kuhl, assistant cashier of the United States Bank, 1793, afterwards cashier of the Farmers' and Mechanics' Bank, occupied the next three-story brick, with its porch in front, where doubtless he often enjoyed the morning air—and the evening breeze, a comfort now repudiated by the refinement of the age.

The next house was a frame, occupied by Leonard Jacoby, the sire of the survivors of that family, previous to 1793; in that year he owned and occupied the corner, vacated by Mr. Wirtz, and there successfully pursued his calling of shipping merchant, in the Dutch and German trade, and who, after business hours, sat "*otium cum dignitate*," enjoying his "knaster" inside his door, through the medium of a very long-shanked German pipe.

A French boarding-house was next adjoining. Afterwards, in 1801, Mrs. Catherine Fisler was an eminent hostess in the same place and occupation.

Mrs. Anna Cook, a bonnet-maker of note, and her husband, George Cook, no less so as a tailor, succeeded a certain Sebastian White, a watchmaker, in the occupancy of the next house, the southeast corner of Coates's Alley; at the northeast corner, John Melbeck held forth as a merchant.

From Coates's Alley northward, there were several frames and small-sized three-story brick houses, in one of which, near the corner of Key's Alley, Joseph Herzog began the grocery business, and at the southeast corner of Key's Alley, was the residence of the late Dr. Ashbel Green, pastor of the Presbyterian Church, then situated, with a very handsome steeple, at the northwest corner of Third and Arch Streets.

This being my limit, and sufficient for the diagraph ot a neighborhood, I shall return on the west side, and lay off that ground, with its possessions, southward to Race Street, as near as possible.

At, or near the corner of New Street, was the office and residence of John Baker, Esq., for many years a justice of the peace, and, a few doors below, a certain George Tryon, a tin-smith and copper-smith.

Simmons's board-yard here occupied a considerable space on Second Street, and extended through to Third Street. George Brown, a tobacconist of note and long standing, exhibited the seductive weed, for a comfortable smoke, next below; whilst the Camel Tavern offered the services of Henry Huber to the wayworn traveller, and its spacious conveniences to retirement of his jaded beast.

This ante-revolutionary relic is still the existing monument of its own fame.

An alley or passage here to the background of the tavern splits the line.

Hood & Wilson, as grocers, start at this south corner, and Philip Wager occupies a large front for his wine store and dwelling. These were first class three-story brick buildings adjoining.

Habacher, a partner of Mr. Wager, fills the space to the yet existing Buck Tavern, kept by George Hill. The grounds of this tavern extended through to Third Street.

David Jones, a hatter, made up the corner of another passage to the rear of Race and Third Street lots. Mr. Jones was a very early resident of that neighborhood.

On the southwest corner of this passage, Edward Randolph, of the subsequent firm of Coates and Randolph, kept a grocery store; and next below, was the residence of Parson Hendel, of the Dutch Presbyterian Church; whose widow, a remarkably kindly-mannered old lady, and her two daughters, kept a queen's-ware store in the same place, for many years after his decease.

Jacob Schreiner, next below, could tell of the loss or gain of the hardware business; whilst his neighbor, Bosbyshell, could light up the vista of the *modus operandi* of the dry goods merchant's arcade; but our ancient friend, Conrad Gerhard, a baker, in those days, was even more appetital in his issues, since, besides the general products of his oven, his helpmeet was popularly *au fait* in the science of cake-baking, whose never-to-be-forgotten Moravian sugar-cake was ever and anon toothsome to the most fastidious epicure.

But here, too, we have a relish for social epicurianism in the person and character of a certain Tobias Hirte.

This specimen of the olden time was resident in the second story of the back building of No. 118, just named.

He was a bachelor, an itinerant apothecary, a hermit, or a cit, as fancy or convenience might suggest.

His itinerancy was not limited to the mere disposing of curatives, nor the single eye to gain. He was fond of travel. "Liberty and independence was his motto;" and when mounted on his sorrel mare, with saddle-bags at each side, and a large umbrella, with a handle of unusual length, on the pommel of his saddle, he bestrode the pinnacle of his glory; and the summer season, from early spring, opened the highway to this enjoyment.

Although vending his compounds as he passed the route of his search, his principal object, for many years, was a visit to the Indians—Seneca, and several other tribes—with whom he was on the most sociable terms, and whose chiefs always called on him, at his hermitage in Philadelphia, when they came.

Amongst these were Cornplanter, the Seneca Chief, and his associate, Red Jacket, both of whom I have seen in his room in Second Street, and before whom, some sixty years ago, perched on a chair, I was encouraged to repeat a verse, as taught me by this noble Indian, beginning thus:

Jesus mil u ner, Toma Tima na,
Ipse woolaa den a waagen, &c. &c.

Being the Seneca version of,

"Jesus, hear our prayer,
Take of us good care," &c.

Cornplanter was a noble specimen of our race, in person and purpose, and known to history as a very efficient aid to General Washington. He died on the 7th of February, 1836, on the Seneca Reservation, in Pennsylvania, at the age of about one hundred years.

Thus associated, my subject was facilitated in his gatherings of social, as well as pecuniary wealth, and his sale of Seneca oil made him as popular as his details of Indian customs, manners, and peculiarities; the special purpose of his annual visit being to gather or purchase this oil from the Senecas.

Although an itinerant, he was not without homes, seeing that the interim of his travel found him at—what he called—his country seat, in Lebanon, Pa., where he cultivated and enjoyed fruits of all kinds, and the most choice.

Apples, pears, peaches, plums, apricots, nectarines, watermelons, and cantelopes, all yielded to him the most grateful sense of their culture and existence, and the rise and progress of which he could scan from the back door of his cabin, as he rested from the perusal of his "Aurora," a Democratic daily paper of that day, and adjusted his "specs" for another political treat. The approach of winter, however, dismantled his forest of luxuries; and his closed doors, shutting out all nature, the city was his last resort, and to the city he came to make, prepare, decoct and concoct cures or palliatives for all the ills common to man!

Here, in a room of about ten by fifteen feet, sat this veteran in nostrums, picturesque in the adornment of his walls with the remains of a music store, fiddles, flutes, French horns, and the like; whilst below, in one corner, stood an old-timed spinnet, steadied to the floor by a fifty-six pound weight on its lid or top, in range of which sat the "lord of his survey," at a table either redolent of roast goose, apple-sauce, &c., or a mass of pill-stuff, or other medicament, in preparation of a summer's trip; whilst behind him sat a boy, bottling or boxing curatives for all the ills of human inheritance, spurred to speed by the promise of a feast of coffee and sugar-cake at the end of the week. In front stood a large and very grand—as we thought in those days—mantle clock; but, a little beyond, another, of more importance and more interest. This was a musical clock—a great curiosity; whose Swiss peasantry, in a recess over the dial, took an hourly turn in a cosy dance, to the jingle of a most fascinating set ot well-tuned bells; gazed and wondered at by the Schuank-felders, who supplied him regularly on the evenings of Tuesday and Friday, with cream, butter, and Dutch cheese; the latter always most popular for its offensive odor.

He was a bachelor to all intents and purposes, and his apartment a stranger to whisk or water. His habits were unique. He prepared and ate his breakfast of toast and coffee, at about 10 A.M.; lunched on tea and toast, or plain bread and butter, and Dutch cheese, at 2 P.M.; but dined sumptuously on roast pig (which he called "span-ferkle"), or roast goose, with no small amount of potatoes, apples, cold-slaw, bread and butter, &c., settled with seve ral glasses of good Madeira, at about 11 o'clock at night, and then a pipe; and then, despite Homœopathy, if all within was of doubtful temperament, a goodly number o

Von Swieten's pills—a composition principally of aloes —were sent to check rebellion. Yet he killed the time of near one hundred years.

In his room, a large drab great-coat covered the imperfections of a patch on his trowsers, or a modicum of snuff on the sleeves or the bosom of his shirt.

Saving his choice of celibacy, he was a man of good sound sense; content with the fruits of his daily labor, which he interspersed with reading, writing, and arithmetical calculations on the waste of time by minutes, &c.; for the rest, his maxim was to eat when hungry, drink when thirsty, and sleep when weary; and so he did; reserving the latter, however, for a pillow-review of his authorship, penned whilst the

> "Drowsy world lay lost in sleep,
> Or nought stirred rudely;"

for he seldom retired before two o'clock in the morning; nevertheless, his Sabbath was not infringed by his anticipation of its earlier hours, but on the contrary, 10 A.M. and 3 P.M. found him in his chair in the choir of the church, which his *pizzicato* and *fortenuto* very soon announced; and he it was, on whose infirmity compassion shone, to melt his infliction in a compromise of brotherly forbearance.

He departed this life in the month of April, 1833, at what he was wont to call his country seat, at Lebanon, Pa.

Leaving this ancient friend and his Indian associates in the shades of their final rest, but with a respectful reminiscence of their existence, I pass on to the line of my project, and present the next in order, the northwest corner of Second and Race Streets.

This lot was the tavern yard, with the necessary supply of sheds, stables, &c., appurtenant to a hostelrie.

This property was purchased by the sire, Mr. Abraham Wilt, who raised the corner to three stories, put up back buildings on Race Street, and a full-sized three-story brick house and store on the vacant lot on Second Street, where he continued and ended his business pursuits, and built for his retirement the present three-story brick house on the extreme end of the corner lot, where he also finished his mortal career.

The corner was occupied, early in the present century, by C. Bernanos, grocer, and afterwards by P. M. Lafourcade, a printer.

The west corner of the four-feet passage just described was the residence of Mrs. Catharine Roman,* a German gentlewoman, of kindly suavity of manner.

She was the mother-in-law of the late Capt. Daniel Man, who married her only daughter, but who died at a very early period of her life.

The next house is a twin to the one below, doubtless both built at the same time, and far in the last century. It was the book-bindery of John R. and Godfrey Baker.

The adjoining wide front and more modern style, covers the site of more ancient honors, a Friend's school-house once having dignified the spot, and perpetuated its fame and its identity by a permanent ground-rent, a tribute to its memory, of $144 per annum, payable to the Friend's Society.

* This old lady departed, April 29th, 1812, upwards of 80 years of age. She was present at the laying of the corner-stone of our first Moravian Church, a contemporary of Count Zinzendorff, and heard him preach in Germantown, was a member of his society, and lived and died a full member of the Church. (Extract from the Church Register.)

Matthias Keely occupied the new house for several years as a merchant; and Mr. John R. Baker afterwards was the owner and occupant, pursuing the German trade and the sale of some German books. John Nicholas Seidel, currier, preceded Mrs. Barnes, in the two-story blue frame above, who was there, for many years, an eminent bonnet-maker.

A one-story building yet fills the next lot, once said to be a gambling resort, but subsequently respectably appropriated by John Jacob Sommer, well-known to the German community as an importer of German linens; a very polite, and, at that time (German), bachelor.

Now passing the King of Prussia, and Piesch and Mayerhoff—peace to their memory, a clever pair.—I pass onwards, and a one-story frame offers its claims to perpetuity, as it once offered its services to the building fraternity, at the hands of Mr. Frank Engles, ironmonger.

Old Thomas Williams, a very venerable and communicable Quaker gentleman, occupied the next three-story brick for many years, and prospered there in his business of cabinet-making, so that he purchased the adjacent one-story frame, and built a full-sized three-story brick on the lot.

Mr. Williams was born and brought up in Fourth Street near Ranstead Court, then called Rutter's Alley, from the, perhaps, earliest tenant of that *locale*, George Rutter—more properly, however, Ritter—that being the original family name.

He has often told me of his boyhood, and the circumscribed boundary of the city, in his early day, of vacant lots, from the head of the court, or alley, to Fifth Street, and the gathered youth there imbibing religious instruction on the Sabbath, or venting their redundant spirit in juvenile sports on week holidays.

He departed this life, on the 25th day of February, 1846, in the 83d year of his age.

The next house, a two-story brick, was the dwelling and cedar-coopering establishment of Mr. Jacob Rees, identified by time and occupation with that neighborhood.

Daniel Zeller exhibited his calling as grocer in the next two-story brick; the house still telling of long life by its wrinkles, its rust, and its waste.

Next, west of this, there were two very old red frames, one of which was the early bread bakery of Mr. Jacob Churr, probably both.

Mr. Churr afterwards (1810) occupied and continued his business in the three-story brick, next west of the frames, until his retirement. He is still living, in his 90th year, and in very good health.

In 1795, the property was occupied by Melchior Steiner, printer, but afterwards, in 1801, it was the tavern and head-quarters of the "Tammany Society," whence, if real Indians did not come, they were made to order, of which the host, Valentine Burkhardt, furnished some specimens of real life; but the general issue from that centre was as natural as a veritable Cherokee or Choctaw, and vastly interesting to us young folks.

But here, adjacent, we have certainly an ante-revolutionary structure; and, doubtless, a contemporary of Zinzendorff's Moravian Church.

This building was about forty feet square, two and a half stories high, and supposed to be the first German Reformed Church in this city.

It was purchased and altered into two dwellings by

—— Ball. Philip Wager, the elder, occupied the one as a biscuit bakery; but Mr. John R. Baker and Godfrey Haga afterwards purchased the property, and raised it to three stories, as it now stands, and lived in it. It was, however, previously appropriated to the vile purposes of a gambling-house.

The evidence of this original fixture is first the two feet front and back walls, yet standing, and the large door and massive key once in the actual possession of Mr. John R. Baker, besides the traditionary revelations of our fathers.

Our old and respectable townsman, John Singer, occupied the next.

Jacob Lawerswyler owned the next; and the late Lewis Rush exhibited the evidence of his profession, as skin-dresser, by a sheet of parchment from the third house.

The three houses yet stand against the waywardness of modern fancy.

The northeast corner of Third and Race Streets an old time two and three-quarter storied brick building, with hip, or broken roof, belonged to the Coates family, and was occupied by Thomas Coates, the sire of that generation, as a grocery store.

These details show up Race Street, from Second to Third Street, a highly respectable business location, quite equal to Market Street, in that early day. It lapsed for a time, but now again seems to be recuperating. We must, however, turn the corner, and call up the manes of things that were in that direction.

CHAPTER III.

Review of Third Street, from Race Street, northward, to New Street, East Side; and West Side, southward, to Race Street.

Leaving Coates's grocery at the corner, we pass several small-sized three-story brick dwellings, old, rusty, and original; the two northernmost yet standing, one of which was occupied by a certain Mary Sellers, widow, a schoolmistress; the other by Nicholas Coleman, a baker; afterwards by Mrs. Weiss, whose mart for gingerbread, candies, &c., was a toothsome temptation to the hot penny of neighboring and passing children; they are still there. An eleven-feet passage here divides the line, placing two other tenements, of like kith and kin, on the north side of the passage; but these have long since given way and place to the wholesale grocery house of Messrs. Jordan & Brother, the successors of the next in order.

Here, No. 123, marks the choice spot of the late Godfrey Haga, for the erection of a store and mansion of 1792. A very spacious, first class, three-story brick building adorned this neighborhood; for, by comparison, it was by far the most extensive arrangement for business, as well as domestic accommodations, in that square, *i. e.*, Third from Race to Vine Streets.

The lot was thirty-four feet in front, a part of which was an arched and paved cartway, to appropriate back stores, over which the upper part of the building extended.

The firm of Boller & Jordan, grocers, opened here, and continued till the death of Frederick Boller, in 1802, dissolved the partnership; and the business was continued by Mr. Jordan, afterwards, in association with Samuel Worman, under the firm of Jordan & Worman; and subsequently, until the maturity of his sons, by Mr. Jordan alone.

The dwelling part of this building was the domicile of Mr. J. Jordan until 1845, when the frost of many winters bore down ambition, and silenced the spirit that erewhile gave life and tone to earlier scenes. The germ, however, sprouted, and the rising generation of his house, in successful operation, meeting the exigencies of the times, laid waste the gatherings of the last century, and spread their card of invitation to popular fancy in more modern form; where, even now, hardware, crockery, &c. &c., are offered for sale, instead of sugar, coffee, tea, &c. &c.

The lot adjoining the old house and store, was the rear end of the Buck Tavern lot, and was occupied by D. Zeller, with its very old frame covering of his fish, grindstones, &c.

In 1816, this frame gave place to a full-sized three-story brick house, put up by Mark Richards, who removed there from the opposite (southwest) corner of Branch Street, and continued his trade in bar and pig iron; and where, also, originated his private banking, and the issue of his tickets for small change, from 6¼ cents to $3.

From this point, northward, several of the original buildings remain. But the original Eagle Tavern, with its black-headers, has long since passed to the shades, and remoulded to suit the fancy of modern requirements.

In 1795, it was kept by a certain John Bisbing; afterwards by Henry Haines, the owner of it, and several of the adjoining properties.

The west end of Simmons's board-yard here occupied considerable space—now extensively and very handsomely improved by several capacious four-story stores.

Next above the then board-yard, we have two three-story brick houses, of 1780, built by Thomas Hockley, a miller, and Samuel Garragues, a builder.

Mrs. Hockley, his widow, and her son-in-law, Josiah Twamly, of the firm of Roberts & Twamly, No. 80 Market Street, and the widow Twamly, were successive residents in the corner house, until within a few years. They were all members of Christ Church, and highly respectable from sire to scion. The property remained in the family until very recently, when it—the corner—was sold for $13,000. Its domestic scenes and comforts had long since been usurped by gunny-bags and sugar-hogsheads for the supply of the pantries of other domains.

In passing down the west side of Third from New Street, many of the old buildings remain, and occupancies, little varied from the present time, saving and excepting alterations, to meet the exigencies of extended trade; else hatters, shoemakers, shop-keepers, merchants, and the sea-captain, Casper Foulke, as well as Andrew Bush, the shoemaker of our early day, all flourished there, but the corner was the key of knowledge, in the hands of Joseph Yerkes, a schoolmaster of and previous to 1791, since occupied by Israel Roberts, coppersmith.

The southwest corner of Third and Branch, was the grocery store of Philip Dick, afterwards by Mark Richards, before he built on the opposite side of Third Street.

Dr. Ashbel Green also was resident next below, before he lived in Second Street. (See Chapter II).

Mrs. Sarah, widow of Thomas Bartow, occupied the most modern house of the row, and her widowed daughter, Mrs. Mary Peter, continued there until the bustle of business life suggested a more retired domicile.

Isaac Wampole, a scrivener, preceded our well-known townsman and alderman, John Geyer, Esq.; and John Hay, proprietor of the old Rotterdam Inn, was a fixture of 1791, where the same inducement is still offered for the comforts and conveniences of man and horse, with its open way to the sheds and stables, appurtenant to the establishment. The corner was an old-time three-story brick, with hip roof and gable on Third Street, and lot extending to the south line of the above passage.

It was occupied in 1795 by Charles Erdman, an interpreter and land broker, but for many years afterwards by Jacob Mayland, as a segar manufactory and tobacco warehouse. There was originally a shoemaker-shop on the rear end of this lot, kept by Peter Waggoner, so early as 1791, at or before Erdman's time.

Excepting the "Old Rotterdam," and one or two originals next above this line, from Race to Branch Streets is lost in modern attire, and knows itself no more.

CHAPTER IV.

Race above Third—White Swan—German Reformed Church—Riffert's Tavern—John Warder, &c.—Third below Race—Christian Denckla, Conrad Weckerly, Frederick Bealer, Andrew Leinau, John Heyler Jacob Mayland, Philip S. Bunting.

REMINISCENCE and data together lead me around this corner of Third Street, to gather and review some of the earlier life of that avenue to or near to Fourth Street.

There appears to have been in the days of our fathers, a penchant for foreign taste, fancy, and fashion, seeing that they too had their French hatters, French shoemakers, French boarding-houses, French bathing-houses, French tailors, French brokers, French baker, French hair-dresser, and, in a word, *à la mode de Paris* was enacted at all points; and here on our right hand we have a certain Charles Carri, a French tailor, and a few doors above him, John Anthony and John Baptist Massieu offer the luxuries of a French bathing-house, and for aught we know, a French barber, may have preceded Jacob Sink, or succeeded him, at No. 105, a spot ever memorable and select for a barber's shop; but this No. 105 is absorbed in the present new corner, and 107 exhibits the striped pole appurtenant to the profession.

The very respectable mansion, about midway in the

square, No. 117, now owned and occupied by Mr. John Bacon, is a fixture of 1786, and was occupied, up to 1793, by Henry Epply as a tavern and keeper of horses and chairs.

It was a centre of *tone* and *ton*. The *first* city dancing assembly met here on the "light fantastic toe," patronized by the late Mrs. Wm. Bingham.

General Washington met his companions in arms here, whilst our Indian Seneca chief, Cornplanter, and his vivacious son, mingled with these survivors of battle, and welcomed as their guest and ally the recently unfortunate Louis Philippe.

In 1795, it was the residence of William Nichols, Marshal for the District of Pennsylvania, and about the year 1803–5, became the property and domicile of Mr. John Warder, whose good lady had a soup society of her own, preparing that comfort, and distributing it to the poor, once a week, gratis.

The adjoining lot west was occupied by a frame tenement, in which Cornplanter and his son had their apartment, in Epply's time.

Mr. Bacon, the present owner of the mansion, has given life to the spot for fifty-one years.

A little west of this, No. 131 and 132 fill the space of the hostelrie of Isaac Rich and the widow Winckhouse. The tavern was last kept by —— Rifferts. It had an extensive rear carriage-way from Race Street.

The odor of molasses candy, in all the phases of Strodeck's science, now perfumes the atmosphere that erewhile touched the olfactories with the pungent exhalations from Doctor Budd's apothecary shop, next above, which, in earlier times, was the domicile of Thomas Allibone, the father-in-law of Doctor Budd;—a respectable mansion, and most respectably tenanted.

Vis à vis, we have the old German Reformed Church, the pastorate, in 1795, of the Rev. Mr. Hendel, afterwards of the Rev. Mr. Helffenstein, &c.

It was built on the line of the pavement, ninety feet on Race Street by sixty-five feet deep. The front on Race Street had doors of entrance near the east and west boundaries, and corresponding conveniences of egress and ingress in the opposite or southern wall.

The pedestal pulpit was at the centre of the south wall, the long side of the church; and the organ, a dignified affair, and monument of Tannenberg's skill, answered from its elevation—at the touch of a junior Rev. Beebighaus—the commands of the venerable pastor.

The building has passed to the world of atoms, but again remoulded on the rear of the same lot, retired from the increased noise of the street.

Except the renewed corner of Sterling Alley, antiquity holds its own down to the "White Swan Tavern;" this, too, has been rebuilt, and its tenants over and often renewed; but it was probably the starting-point of George Yohe, who was there in 1797 or 1800, and afterwards famous, through his second wife, Catharine, in the annals of hotel-keeping, for her attraction of the mercantile community, for whom she formed a centre by her location, a very hive for the country merchants; and her memorabilia will long live in the manes of the Washington Hotel, in Fourth, near Market, west side (William Chancellor's house), the Western Hotel, Market below Ninth, south side, and her final enterprise in the purchase of three houses on the south side of Chestnut Street, above

Sixth, and exemplifying her ability by converting them into a large—perhaps the largest—hotel in the city, at the time. The influence of her success created a vastly profitable atmosphere for the mart of her gathering.

But to return. The Swan still marks the spot, and the original stage-office next below, with its arched way to the stables in the rear, yet tells of yawning candidates for a seat in the Bethlehem and Easton stages at 4, and sometimes, when roads were deep, even at 1 o'clock in the morning; and thence, sometimes, till 10 o'clock at night (only twenty years ago) to the place of destination.

The southwest corner of Third and Race was the property of Conrad Weckerly, who kept store in the rear, on Race Street, and whose refractory queue, popping from beneath the collar of his coat, in which his head was well-nigh lost, betrayed its owner, as well as the front that claimed it.

There were three three-story, small-sized brick houses, forming this Third Street line. In one of these, our respectable old German friend, Christian H. Denckla, laid the foundation of a handsome fortune, from the result of his industry in the prosecution of his business as an importer and vender of Nüremberg and other German goods.

A few doors below this, there was a hut of ancient date —a one-story red frame—hugged in by houses of larger growth on either side. This cabin was the hermitage of Frederick Beates, who, in his elbow-chair—as one item—might ever and anon be seen before his table, at the back window, diving into the mysteries of the past for rights, titles, and interests; for the perfection of wills, deeds, bonds, mortgages, and other writings, as they presented their claims to his professional acumen.

Mr. Beates was an old-time scrivener, very determined in his conclusions, and unimpeachably correct in his professional judgment. His services were always desirable, but not always attainable. The integrity of his client was vastly important to the enlistment of his attention; and whether he would or would not, depended much upon the bland and unequivocal offerings to his measure of integrity.

He was *the* scrivener of his day; moderate and merciful in his demands, charitable to the incompetent, and kindly free in his advice.

His early sanctum was sold to Wm. B. Scull, and the site improved, and is now occupied by Spang & Wallace. He moved thence into a small two-story brick, one or two doors below, where, in common parlance—by accident—he closed his useful and very popular career.

Industry, perseverance, and integrity, were cardinal virtues with Mr. Beates, whilst truthful certainty was the pride of his profession.

In pursuance of this desideratum—

> "When all were gone,
> And nought stirred rudely,"

he drew upon the midnight oil to light his way to the secrets of law and musty parchments. But "all things to their period tend." On the night of the 9th of December, 1841, enfeebled by the wear and tear of time, he fell a victim to his ambition; and the flame that lit it, on this unpropitious occasion, also extinguished it by its consuming contact, and set at nought his wonted powers of resistance.

He lingered a few days; departed on the 14th, and was interred in the German Lutheran Burial-ground, on the 16th of December, 1841, in his 80th year. He had been a resident of this neighborhood upwards of sixty years.

Returning northward, on the east side of Third Street, we have Andrew Leinau's hatting establishment, in 1795, at the northeast corner of Quarry Street; and a little beyond, at No. 107, our ancient and modern friend, too, Mr. John Heyler, whose friendly *good a mornen* saluted many a consumer of silk stockings, silk caps, oil cloths, &c., at his door or counter, and begat for him a profitable reputation, even unto the thirteenth or fourteenth year of the present century.

Here, in this region, a traditionary anecdote seems to belong to its history.

The husband of a certain Mrs. L—— departed this life, after a very short illness. The old lady, taken by surprise, and having passed a long life without any previous like affliction, was inconsolable, and at his lifeless side cried aloud, "George! George!" as if to wake him. On being remonstrated with by a friend, she replied, "*O my! O my! I never saw him so before!*"

Passing this digression, we note the starting-point of Jacob Mayland, tobacconist, who afterwards, for many years, was the active and efficient proprietor of the store, northwest corner of Third and Race, already noted.

The two-story frame, hedged in by grindstones on its outer walls, but full fledged, in its inner, with sugar, coffee, tea, &c., all the important appendages of a grocery store, kept by Philip S. Bunting, 1793, made up the southeast corner.

This row, from Quarry to Race, has but one specimen of the olden time remaining, a single wrinkle of the face that once identified the spot.

Returning from this corner down the south side of Race, to our place of beginning, the tooth of time yet marks its prey, presenting, for the most part, the façade of nearly one hundred years' wear and tear; but Mr. William Wood pursues his calling of tailor, in connection with his gentlemen's furnishing establishment, on or next below the spot of his birth and the homestead of his parents, of the last century. Nos. 90 and 92, marked these possessions.

Anthony Vitry, an unassuming little Frenchman, of very measured pace, exhibited epaulets and other military ornaments at the window of No. 88. A certain E. P. Aublay, a French citizen, occupied the premises before.

Passing Elizabeth Neelan, a shopkeeper, at No. 86, we come to the present Green House, a tavern, and call to mind an earlier and vastly uneasy spirit, who paced the pave, under the windows of the parlor, the width of the front, to and fro, all day, and every day, for several years, a segar alone being his constant boon companion.

Seth Robinson had been a sailor, and perhaps, under illusion, continued to walk the deck of his bark.

His family were occupants here of the last century.

Joanna Gravenstine perfumed the atmosphere with the odor of oranges, lemons, and the savory luxuries of the Torrid Zone.

Two boarding-houses adjoining complete the line to Moravian Alley.

But the memory of our present respectable friend and citizen, Jacob Fritz, is a ray of the Revolution, and the key of that block, seeing that his father, John Fritz, was resident at that corner, in 1780, in the same house, the shoulder of the square.

Mr. Jacob Fritz is now in his eightieth year; a good sample of industry and steady habits, a gentleman of the old school.

His father, John Fritz, was the pioneer publican of No. 85, on the opposite side, afterwards successively continued by Rifferts & Burkhardt, and till very recently by Mr. Jacob Churr, baker.

In the early part, and for many years, of this century, this corner of Moravian Alley was occupied by John Stow, a tinner, whose shop was in the rear, fronting on the alley.

CONCLUSION.

A Stray Chapter, comprising a View from Second to Front Streets, and a Review of Second, from Drinker's Alley to Arch Street, East and West Side, with Sketches of Character of some of the Life of that Section.

ALTHOUGH the volume might have closed with the last chapter, recollections seem to forbid the truce, and appeal to patience for a further hearing, which may not be altogether uninteresting to the present, as well as to future generations.

The sunken cities of Pompeii and Herculaneum have been, and are even yet being explored, and the cement of Vesuvius mined, over all its fatal embrace, to discover the march of mind of their day; nor life, limb, health, and wealth, are ever a consideration for the desideratum. Now, although *our* city may not be subject to a like catastrophe, her vast domains must evaporate, in fractions, to oblivion unexplorable, but for the gathering of its parts by antiquarian spirits, as time and circumstances remove its identity. With this view of both ends of time, the impetus of recollection is irresistible, and the neighborhood of the old Church seems to claim a further development.

Taking, therefore, another turn, and leaving the northeast corner of Second and Race Streets, eastward, there are yet two three-story old-style brick houses, in one of which—early in the present century—lived Dr. John

Perkin, and in the other, Mr. Andrew Fenton, a very popular ladies' shoemaker.

Jackson's Court here broke the line, and ran northward to or near Brooks's Court, which opened on Front above Race Street.

This passage, with an old frame on the lower corner, was purchased by the late Capt. Daniel Man, and improved by him, by a large three-story brick mansion, with side-lot, gate, garden, and counting-house in the rear, whose walls, could they speak, might echo instructions to the unwary dealer in discounts and deposits, and "teach the young idea how to shoot."

This mansion is now the resort for hunger and thirst of a different sort; and a restaurant and lager beer saloon absorbs what else was gathered on that spot.

For the rest, the face of this row has been but slightly altered. The residences of Abraham Woglom, bricklayer, John Willis, clerk in the Navy Agency of the late George Harrison, Dr. Glentworth, Capt. Hedelius, Capt. Strong, Andrew Simmons, a silversmith, and some half dozen other respectable two-story brick specimens of the olden time, still identify the spot of their former tenants.

The south side of this square has paid a heavier tribute to modern fancy. The counting-houses and domiciles of J. B. Foussat and John F. Dumas, *vis-à-vis* Capt. Man, with their busy tenants, have passed Time's ordeal, and their memory also lost.

The retired cabin, a two-story frame, with its sombre pent-house, some sixty feet back from the line, with its well-arranged garden, flanked by a foot-path neatly and mechanically set with clam-shells, once the comfortable quarters of the late Capt. Stevens, is now superseded by

No. 26, and not a shadow left of such an existence; whilst the compounding of simples, and the gentle tones of the pestle and mortar of Jesse Thomson,—midway in the square, at the lower corner of a court—still extant, no longer offers its services to the invalid, or its curative to the hastened messenger from the threatened chamber. They are gone, though they

> "Haunt me still, though many a year has fled,
> Like some wild melody."

But, no thanks to this "wild melody" for some dignified representatives of the olden time there are yet several relics frowning upon modern intrusion, in some half-dozen fixtures, though darkened, yet strengthened by the blasts of near a century's powers, looking askance at their neighbors, and claiming the honors due to longevity.

This sketch of the early appearance of the environs of the original Moravian Church, is no less interesting for its traditionary and mnemonic gatherings than for its facts and data; yet, errors excepted, it is entitled to credit; because the disruption of landmarks, the lack of observation in some of our contemporaries, and the failure of memory in others, throw us upon our own resources; whilst remembrance must be courted for its treasures, either in our own, or the fastnesses of the few octogenarians of antiquarian wealth, even yet rejuvenating in the verdure of youthful recollections; and but for such, the knowledge of the creation itself would have been lost to mortal ken.

If, therefore, my resources have played me false in dots or lines, the facts remain, and history has its tribute; for, depend upon it, reader, although the last hundred years have not entirely swept the course of this *localie*, the next fifty will not leave "one stone upon another" of its present possessions.

But to carry out my plan, I must return to Second Street, and call up the various links of the line from Lawerswyler's to Arch Street, and back on the east side to Drinker's Alley.

Morris's Brewery is of ante-revolutionary origin, and here presents itself as No. 86.

The lot was originally granted by William Penn to Richard Warroll, in 1684, for the consideration of two shillings sterling, per annum; it was fifty-five feet on Second Street by three hundred feet deep, extending across Moravian Alley, not then opened.

In 1741, it was conveyed to Anthony Morris, and remained in that family upwards of one hundred years, and until the enterprise of our townsman, Robert Newlin, made him successor, not only in the business, but in the absolute ownership of the estate.

Mr. Newlin purchased the estate in September, 1848, and by indomitable perseverance has accumulated a large fortune, together with an enviable reputation for the skill, the tact, and the talent, and "*fiat justitia ruat cœlum*," the pleasant open manner that always wins more than it loses.

Besides all this—and that might be enough for one generation—Mr. Newlin holds it with all its antique gatherings.

This brew-house was the rendezvous of the British, where red jackets associated and concocted plans to reduce rebellion to submission, and whence, too, they found it convenient to depart and seek better protection than their promises had performed. Here, too, is affixed the *very first* trophy of Franklin's discovery of conducting the destructive discharge of the electric fluid harmless into the earth; his first lightning rod yet invites its safe conduit from its birth to its burial, in this building.

Next below was the sugar refinery of David Schaeffer, the grandsire of the present cashier of the Girard Bank. Mr. Schaeffer was a Whig in the Revolutionary War, and was, of course, a mark for the vengeance of the enemy; and they *did* vent their opposition by destroying every vestige of manufacturing convenience and appliance, leaving but the bare walls and the floors to advertise their destructive presence.

Muhlenberg & Schaeffer, and in 1795, Morgan, Douglass, & Schaeffer, afterwards continued the business; and later, Piersol & Schaeffer.

The sugar-house was on the rear of Second Street, on Moravian Alley, and accessible by a four or five feet passage, lettered on each wall, first, Muhlenberg & Schaeffer, and again, Piersol & Schaeffer, with a hand pointing to the establishment.

This property is now also a part of the estate of Mr. R. Newlin, by purchase, and forms a part of his extensive brewery, and increases his domains one hundred and thirty feet in depth by eighty-two feet in width.

I do not, however, intend to compile a directory, and therefore must pass jewellers, gentlefolks, and barristers-at-law, &c., to pay our respects to the memory of the venerable Christian gentleman, Mr. John Aitken, of this neighborhood, who from conscientious motives, although a poor man, positively refused to engrave the portrait of Voltaire, for, as he said, an infidel book.

He was an engraver and dealer in music, as was advertised by his implements and samples of his handiwork, displayed in the small bulks at each side of his door. This is the same Mr. Aitken noted in the body of this work.

He departed this life on the 5th of September, 1831, in the 87th year of his age, a godly, righteous, and a sober man.

A few doors below Mr. Aitken, we have an old (original) two-story frame, occupied by —— Woodruff as a grocery store; and next below this my old friend and very suavitous neighbor, Mr. Burton, of No. 66, in those days, a plain, unsophisticated old gentleman, offering his well-assorted stock of queensware, without bore or bolstering, and accomplishing his purpose to a respectable issue.

But now permit me to present my own debut in life's busy theatre, the house and its occupants of No. 64.

This was the property and domicile of Dr. Benjamin Jay, a well-known physician of his day; but immediately after him, was the residence and business place of the Rev. Thomas Dunn.

Mr. Dunn was a divine of the Presbyterian faith, but had no pastoral charge in Philadelphia, save that of an occasional offering from the pulpit of the Tabernacle, then situate at the head of Ranstead Court, Fourth below Market, in the absence or to the relief of its proper pastor, Dr. Hay.

His secular calling was mercantile, and silk and satin ribbons, Dunstable hats, chip and straw bonnets, silk and satin, morocco and kid skins, &c., were bought and sold extensively at his hands.

His spring and fall importations from England, were generally passed off with their season, and that without any garniture of his truthful yea and nay. "Don't tell a lie," was his command; and firm consistency in him was the exemplar, carrying out his principle, with friend or foe. Thus, honest in all his purposes, he could not be beguiled by sophistry, deceit, or hypocrisy; and hence his prompt repudiation of the unfortunate malfeasance of Dr. Hay, in his pastorate, his intimate friend, but whose specious defence, was not permitted to reach and soil his purer sensibilities; and he withstood him to the face, and resisted him to exposure and expulsion.

In 1809, he retired to Germantown, where he took charge of the church standing eastward from the mid-way or six mile toll-gate; but finally retired to Newport, R. I., where he deceased, on the 15th of April, 1833, aged 70 years.

There must be some amongst us yet, who in mental retrospect can read the burden of our window shutters, announcing Thomas Dunn, late Dunn & Bowering, a former partner in New York, as the vender of Dunstables, &c., as well as a glimpse of the sunburnt specimen of flats, swinging or flirting in the wind.

Next below, we have the residence and tailor's trimmings establishment of Newbury Smith. This was a handsome and commodious three-story brick house, with private entrance, store door and window in the lower front. The store was small, but neat and clean as a parlor, and always in order.

The whole lot was twenty-eight by upwards of a hundred feet deep; and the house being twenty feet front, left a side entrance to the rear, of eight feet, giving an open view to his prettily arranged garden.

Mr. Smith was a most even-tempered, mild Quaker gentleman, whose early industry and frugality ripened a competency for the protection of a frosted brow, to which time and good health passed him, and under which he enjoyed the comforts of that protection to a good old age.

His was a quiet, peaceable family; children playful, but noiseless; neighborly kindness always free, which none could have experienced more than his neighbor Dunn. "Neighbor Smith," "Neighbor Dunn," and "Neighbor Burton," were a familiar trio, of the most kindly and respectful association; and it is but a small tribute to their memory to say so here, for such may safely be epitaphed:

"Sic transit gloria mundi."

Mr. Smith departed this life on the 1st of September, 1848, aged 87 years.

The clumsy bulk next door, filled with German wares, snuff-boxes, toys, sleigh-bells, Sneeberg snuff, and the whims and oddities of German invention, was in rusty contrast with the domains of Mr. Smith; but its proprietor, *debutant* in business-life, was remarkable for neatness in apparel and gentlemanly deportment. And the reputed handsome German (*Tyroler*), Joseph Ch. Sprenger, lost nothing by the temptation to a passing belle, as his sortie caught the willing glance.

Prosperity took him by the hand and led him on to fortune; but outliving his times, his tact and talent were unequal to the hasty and varied drift of business vicissitudes, and he fell a victim to the mockery of his former ability for any emergency.

The tide that carried him to the upper business circle of Philadelphia, and still onward through the more tempting streams of New York, and yet onward, offered him New Orleans and Texas as playthings, as though mad at its patronizing course, returned him to its ebb, with unmitigated force, to battle with the overwhelming ills of bankruptcy; shorn of the power that blights the scowl of contempt, or that won the smile that erewhile greeted his presence.

Unequal to the reverse, he abandoned the business world, in the spring of 1840, and hid himself from the chilling recognition of the purse-worshipping throng. Shakspeare says, "There is a tide in the affairs of men, if taken at the flood, leads on to fortune." True, very true; but it too often sweeps him back to *mis*fortune, when the dregs of life are reached, and the energies of body and mind are wasted in the sere and yellow leaf.

Beware of this tide, young man; and if it carry you to its bounds, make fast your bark, stay proceedings, and thank God for your footing. Let "well enough" alone.

This reverse, however painful in its disclosure, is but a parenthesis in Time's annals, truly claiming our sympathies, but also warning us against the uncertainty of riches. "If they increase, set not your heart upon them," says the Psalmist; and such events are dark masses in the picture of life. There are, however, rainbow tints of gold and purple in the picture, and they relieve the sombre basis of its background; and such is a tint before us, as we pass onwards.

Moses Bartram, well worn of time, yet an active little

Quaker gentleman, was a kindly available figurante of our neighborhood, and as a dispenser of curatives, gave —by his pestle and mortar—tone, and tune, too, to his seat of customs, where *medicamente*, at his hands, were always *safe* to the invalid, if not even sure to his purpose.

Nor were the tall slim bulks that flanked the limited aperture to his platform, obnoxious to his popularity, or repulsive to his thrift. The spot that knew him, knew him well; seeing that he was always there, under Franklin's motto, "mind your business;" and where thus identified, the direction to "Moses Bartram's apothecary shop, in Second near Arch," soon found itself with the prescription on his counter.

To all appearance, he passed Time's ordeal without the care of much wealth, or the risk or fear of bankruptcy; and shed his mortality under oriental tints of an unclouded sunset.

This was a very old-fashioned small three-story brick house, of ancient date.

The corner, if not of twin birth, was not far behind its neighbor in character and claims of respect for its hoary bearing.

It was a two and a half story brick, occupied by Francis Tete, a Frenchman, and family; but, after his time, was supplanted by a full-sized three-story brick store, and occupied, for many years, as a wholesale grocery, by the late Thomas Reeves, a very clever man, of happy mien, industry, and business capacity, but who was called from the busy scenes of this life, trustful, to a better, before time had passed him from the *comptoir* to the relish of rest from the drudgery of continuous merchandising.

Now, reader, although I do not mean to *cross* the street, we may *look* over at the old and well-known "George Tavern," and scan the jolly Bacchus swung from the corner, high in mid air, astride his keg, attractive to the eye, and, perhaps, inducive to the thirst of a *passing* thought, or soliloquizing wight, on the merits of a well-edged beverage.

As early as 1795, this was the tavern and stage-office of Robert Bicknell, well known, in those days, to travellers to and from New York and Baltimore.

The "George Tavern," as such, has long since lost its charms; but the ancient pile is there, and frowns with age upon the youthful usurpation of its neighboring soil, accompanied in its scowl by its early contemporary, at the southeast corner, of antique structure, once, some threescore years and more ago, owned and occupied by Samuel Walker, grocer, then a respectable and desirable residence, "in good order and well conditioned,"—now, however, shredding to the gatherings of time to darken the clouds of oblivion.*

The northeast corner of Arch and Second was certainly an ante-revolutionary fixture, but extant in our time.

An old two-story red frame was the burden of this nook, but though of humble bearing, was the soil of richer growth; and, perhaps, the very nucleus of opulence.

It was of the estate of William and John Monington, conveyed to Charles Moore, the grandfather of our townsman, the late Henry Pratt, in May, 1751, who became owner afterward, and there opened on the world with the sale of crockery, queensware, and the like.

* This building is even now (June, 1857) being supplanted by a modern idea.

The golden harvest to Mr. Pratt, in after life, is a proud triumph of industry, perseverance, and good manners, and a winning encouragement to patience, and a faithful attention to business, by "he that by the plough would thrive."

The most of the houses northward to Drinker's Alley, hold up their storm-worn faces, and even yet contrast with a very few intrusions of modern date; there are, however, incidents and personal associations that belong to this locality.

It is said that Talleyrand de Perigord, during part of his exile, kept a shop for the sale of buttons in this neighborhood. He was at that time very poor, and also lived for a time in Goddard's Alley, above Vine Street.

His house, pointed out to me when I was a boy, was the southern corner of an arched way to certain back stores, occupied later by Bolton, as and for a hatter shop.

Passing Benjamin Leedom, merchant, at the opposite corner, we have another terror to evil-doers, under the aldermanic powers of Michael Hillegas; an incident of whose times may not be uninteresting in contrast with the growth and perfection of science.

The mysteries of animal magnetism, called *pow-wowing*, &c., were even then, in 1780–1790, hidden in doubtful disputations; yet, there were those who felt its force, and believed in its virtues, but not possessed of scientific skill, would practise, but could not fully perform. Of such, the parent of your writer, then a young man, was one, the elder Samuel Wetherill another, and a third, not recollected.

Doubtful as to the result of their experiments, they *would* try them, and exercising their skill upon a young female, put her to sleep, but could not wake her up, which creating an alarm, they were arrested, and taken before Esquire Hillegas, where innocence of harmful intention was admitted as a plea, but threats of condign punishment for a repetition ended their further curiosity.

My father was also threatened with a suit for *shocking* a man with his electrical machine, who denounced its force as the "black art," after calling him to the outside of the door to advise him to abandon the association.

This man flew at the shock, tore off the connection, swore that it had "lightened," ran down stairs, and did not stop till he was clear of the front door, when he returned and tapped at the window, to make his threat, and give his advice.

This No. 90 North Second Street was afterwards the residence of our highly respected citizen-merchant, Mr. Joseph Clark, who also occupied the back stores just named, for the storage of merchandise. Mr. Clark was extensively engaged in the South American trade, but the uncontrollable blasts of adversity beat down the bulwarks of his most strenuous exertions, and exposed his declining life to the discomforts and inconvenience of an empty treasury; but despite all this, he was no less respectable after than before, and yielded to the wise providence of God, even to the end of life, with that fortitude which was the evidence of a "good profession, before many witnesses."

Nor can I pass this gentleman without a complimentary notice of his kind and gentle housekeeper, Mrs. Carr, who served him in that capacity for many years, and showed as clean a front as Second Street could boast of, as well in person as profession.

The Mount Vernon House covers the site, with some

additions to its breadth, of the late Philip S. Bunting, who removed there, from the southeast corner of Third and Race Streets; whilst Elfrith's Alley still shows up the shoulders that erst marked the line of this passage.

Jeremiah Elfrith and —— Gilbert, his brother-in-law, were proprietors of much of the soil of this avenue, and it bore the name of Elfrith's, or Gilbert's Alley for a long time.

In or about the year 1780, Mr. Elfrith was resident on Second Street, about midway to Drinker's Alley. His house stood back, having a garden or lawn in front; the lot was deep, and formed an L, opening on to Elfrith's Alley.

John Angue was no small consideration to the epicure, in "*Noyau*" "*Parfait Amour*," "*Anise*," and the various oozings of a scientific distillery.

He was a popular French gentleman, and his very relishable emollients passed and extended his popularity through many and various circles of the *beau monde*.

Although he, and his nephew successor, recently offering the same temptations, at old No. 30, North Third Street, have long since passed to the monumental mound, the full-sized senior, with his snuff-box in hand, will doubtless be fresh in the minds of many of the contemporaries of his day,—about the year 1800, and for some years after.

The southeast corner of Drinker's Alley was rebuilt, many years ago, with its present first class two-story brick house, by Isaac Hazlehurst, Esq., for a residence; having his counting-house a short way down the alley.

John Jacob Sommer, of Race Street, having married, afterwards became the occupant of these premises, and held them for many years.

But here I must cease my wanderings, my bounds being already overleapt; but my plan, more extensively carried out, I trust will not be the less acceptable.

Time, fancy, and circumstances have changed the face of this circuit; and recollection and tradition unite with data to portray the review of "the things that were."

But the wisdom of our city fathers has done even more to efface the vestiges of the olden time; and, ere long, there will *not be a single number* to locate a venerated spot, reminiscent of the social or business doings of our *early* fathers; nor can I conceive of any plan to preserve this important directory of ancient landmarks.

Useless, however, as it may seem, whatever numbers I have given, are original numbers, and are traceable by description or comparison.

But, it is as useless to quarrel with the march of improvement. It *will* ride roughshod over every sacred tie of preceding existence. Even the very names of our streets have fallen a prey to a thirst for fame or immortalization, whilst the renumbering even now confuses confusion, and, in time to come, will so confound identity, that old Philadelphia will be a stranger to itself.

But I have done, and *my* part—however limited—of protective recollections, and historical as well as social links, is before you.

My authorities are venerable, truthful, and reliable, whilst my own observation is ably and respectably supported, and warrants me in offering the volume for a modicum of the kindly considerations of the lovers of historical gatherings.

THE END.

ERRATA.

P. 142.—4th line from the top, for "saving," read "seeing."

P. 239.—In foot-note, read "Sarah Quary," instead of "Sarah Quarry."

P. 243.—Read the last paragraph, "This corner," &c., in connection with the foot-note.

P. 266.—13th line from the top, for "Rifferts and Burkhardt," read "Rifferts and Burchartz."

" 2d line from the bottom, for "John Stow, tinner," read "John Stow, turner."

P. 272.—11th line from the bottom, for "Jay," read "Say."

On Plate, "Church and Parsonage," instead of "Race Street," in brackets, read "Bread Street."

On Plate, "Church of 1820," instead of "(now Race Street) and Race Street," read "now Bread and Race Streets."

www.ingramcontent.com/pod-product-compliance
Lightning Source LLC
LaVergne TN
LVHW020221110826
845151LV00003B/780